Journalism in the United States

Concepts and Issues

EDD APPLEGATE

THE SCARECROW PRESS, INC.
Lanham • Toronto • Plymouth, UK
2011

Published by Scarecrow Press, Inc.
A wholly owned subsidiary of The Rowman & Littlefield Publishing Group, Inc.
4501 Forbes Boulevard, Suite 200, Lanham, Maryland 20706
http://www.scarecrowpress.com

Estover Road, Plymouth PL6 7PY, United Kingdom

British Library Cataloguing in Publication Information Available

Library of Congress Cataloging-in-Publication Data

Applegate, Edd.
 Journalism in the United States : concepts and issues / Edd Applegate.
  p. cm.
 Includes bibliographical references and index.
 ISBN 978-0-8108-8185-3 (hardback : alk. paper) — ISBN 978-0-8108-8186-0 (ebook)
 1. Journalism—United States. I. Title.
 PN4853.A66 2011
 071'.3—dc22   2011007292

Printed in the United States of America

For Eva, Clarice, July, and Carolyn.

To the many wonderful students I have known,
as well as the conscientious faculty members
with whom I have worked over the years.

Contents

Introduction

vii

STATE OF THE MEDIA

Print and broadcast journalism in the United States have changed in recent years as a result of millions of people using the Internet and social media for obtaining some or most of the information they desire. Owners and operators of traditional media realize this. Advertisers realize this as well. Traditional media have seen advertising revenues decline over the past several years. Newspapers, for example, lost 26 percent in advertising revenue in 2009 alone.[1] As a result of newspapers downsizing, thousands of journalists have lost their jobs. Local television stations lost 22 percent in advertising revenue in 2009.[2] Like newspapers, these stations have restructured their newsgathering operations. Network television (primarily ABC, CBS, and NBC) lost 8 percent in advertising revenue in 2009.[3] These networks have not renewed contracts with specific news employees as a result of restructuring their news operations. On the other hand, cable television actually captured more viewers; consequently, cable television's advertising revenue increased 5 percent in 2009.[4] Radio stations lost 22 percent in advertising revenue in 2009.[5] Like newspapers, local television stations, and network television, radio stations have let news personnel go. Magazines lost 17 percent in advertising revenue in 2009.[6] News magazines, in particular, have forced staff members to seek employment elsewhere.

Traditional media—magazines, newspapers, radio, and television—should not focus exclusively on the Internet and social media for the answer to their declining advertising revenues, however. Indeed, online lost 5 percent in advertising revenue in 2009.[7] Besides online losing advertising revenue last year, there is another reason why traditional media should not necessarily consider the Internet and social media as a solution to their economic woes: a recent survey found that only 35 percent of Americans have a favorite news destination online. If the site forced people to pay, then only 19 percent would continue to visit.[8] In short, most Americans are not necessarily loyal to any given medium, whether traditional or nontraditional. Today, most Americans seek news based on topic or event; it does not matter which medium covers the subject. This trend is changing the culture of newsrooms, not to mention the finances of news organizations.[9]

Some may think this change in consumer behavior may cause the demise of traditional media, but this belief is not necessarily true. Like traditional media, new media depend on advertising revenue to exist; yet, new media are struggling to find a formula that generates enough advertising revenue to remain in business. Consequently, new media lack the resources and personnel to generate the news or information that people are interested in receiving. Indeed, according to Nielsen Net Ratings data, 80 percent of the traffic to news and information sites is concentrated at the top 7 percent of sites.[10] Most of these sites are tied to traditional media. Thus, the cutbacks in traditional media are affecting content in nontraditional media.[11] The following ten websites were the most popular websites for news in 2009:

1. Yahoo News
2. MSNBC Digital Network
3. AOL News
4. CNN.com
5. NYTimes.com
6. Google News
7. Fox News
8. ABCNEWS
9. Washingtonpost.com
10. USATODAY.com

These sites, except Yahoo News and Google News, produce some content, although most of their content is edited from the Associated Press and other outside sources. These sites focus mainly on national and international news.[12]

Now, inside every major newspaper newsroom, although these newspapers have cut staff, their reporters are being asked to report for the newspaper and its website as well. As if this is not enough, more reporters are being encouraged to contribute other material, including blogs. Local television stations are doing the same. As a result, journalists are working at more than one job. Yet their salaries have not necessarily increased.

PURPOSE OF THE BOOK

The purpose of this book is to discuss specific concepts and issues that pertain to journalism in the United States and to remind people who are interested in journalism that these concepts and issues are important. Indeed, some of these concepts and issues are the foundation on which American journalism is based. The purpose of the first chapter, "Theories of the Press and the Media in the United States," is to contrast and compare four normative press theories—authoritarianism, the former Soviet-totalitarianism, libertarianism, and social responsibility—and to comment on the operations of the media in relation to each. The purpose of the second chapter, "Freedom of the Press," is to provide reasons supported by evidence for the author's contention that the most basic responsibility of the mass media in the United States is to remain free and to point out problems created by the press that threaten its freedom. The history of the First Amendment is examined as well as government controls such as censorship and government secrecy, among others. The purposes of the third chapter, "The Commission on Freedom of the Press and the New Canons of Journalism," are to discuss through the application of the charges and recommendations of the Commission on Freedom of the Press the degree to which the press is or is not fulfilling the goals set forth in the Canons of Journalism written in 1922 and revised and renamed "Statement of Principles" in 1975 by the American Society of Newspaper Editors (ASNE), as well as the changes between the original and revised versions. The American Society of Newspaper Editors recently changed its name to the American Society of News Editors. The purpose of the fourth chapter, "Factors That Impact News," is to present a definition of news, then examine the structure of the print and broadcast industries. Factors such as the business side of the media, the gatekeeper function, the role of advertising, and the role of public relations are discussed. The purpose of the fifth chapter, "The Concepts of 'News Balance' and 'Objectivity,'" is to discuss the compatibility and/or incompatibility of the concepts of news balance and objectivity. The historical development of these concepts is included, as well as an answer to a common plea found in letters written to editors of daily newspapers: "Just give us the straight news—no comments needed—we'll make up our minds." The purpose of the sixth chapter, "The Purposes of the Media," is to define and discuss the three major functions of the media, discuss the strengths and/or weaknesses of each function, identify the function that is best fulfilled by the media, and identify the function that is least fulfilled by the media. The purpose of the seventh chapter, "Media and Minorities," is to examine what "minority" means, then discuss the depiction of minorities by television and the areas in which the press and television have best served and least served the minorities of the United States. Finally, the chapter examines three complaints that minorities have against the media in the United States. The purpose of the eighth chapter, "The History and Questionable Quality of Journalism Education," is to present a brief history of journalism education, then discuss the questionable quality of journalism education by incorporating comments by journalists who work for various media and educators who teach courses in journalism and mass communications programs. Within the discussion the term "quality" differs in meaning. To editors and other professionals in the field, quality means that a student majoring in journalism or mass communications has a broad liberal arts background, including courses in history, political science, economics, sociology, literature, and English composition. To educators, quality means that a student has a background in journalism, mass communications, and the liberal arts. These definitions are the author's. However, each is substantiated. The discussion includes criticisms by professional members of the media and by educators who teach journalism and mass communications in addition to general comments, an analysis of certain studies pertaining to journalism and mass communications education, and appropriate recommendations.

NOTES

1. Project for Excellence in Journalism and Rick Edmonds, "Newspapers: Summary Essay," www.stateofthemedia.org/2010/newspapers_summary_essay.php (19 March 2010).

2. Project for Excellence in Journalism, "Local TV: Summary Essay," www .stateofthemedia.org/2010/local_tv_summary_essay.php (19 March 2010).

3. Project for Excellence in Journalism, "The State of the News Media: 2010: An Annual Report on American Journalism," www.stateofthemedia.org/2010/printable_ overview_chapter.htm (19 March 2010).

4. Project for Excellence in Journalism, "Cable TV: Summary Essay," www .stateofthemedia.org/2010/cable_tv_summary_essay.php (19 March 2010).

5. Project for Excellence in Journalism, "The State of the News Media: 2010."

6. Project for Excellence in Journalism, "The State of the News Media: 2010."

7. Project for Excellence in Journalism, "The State of the News Media: 2010."

8. Project for Excellence in Journalism, "The State of the News Media: 2010."

9. Project for Excellence in Journalism, "The State of the News Media: 2010."

10. Project for Excellence in Journalism, "The State of the News Media: 2010."

11. Project for Excellence in Journalism, "The State of the News Media: 2010."

12. Project for Excellence in Journalism, "The State of the News Media: 2010."

1

Theories of the Press and the Media in the United States

This chapter contrasts and compares four normative theories of the press—authoritarianism, the former Soviet-totalitarianism, libertarianism, and social responsibility—and comments on the operations of the media in the United States in relation to each.

THEORIES OF THE PRESS

Authoritarianism

This is the first as well as the oldest press theory. The modern press actually began in 1450 into an authoritarian society, according to William L. Rivers, Wilbur Schramm, and Clifford G. Christians.[1] This form of society was characterized by the state being above the individual; that is, the state outranked the individual[2] and decided what was best for him, and the state employed the tools of persuasion to preserve unity of thought and action.[3]

According to Roya Akhavan-Majid and Gary Wolf, "Authoritarianism sees the governing elites as inherently good and wise, while the masses are considered to be ignorant and incapable of independently discerning the truth."[4]

Denis McQuail claimed, "What is called 'authoritarian theory' is really a description of two or more centuries of control of the press by various (mostly European) repressive regimes."[5] During the Renaissance, authoritarianism was upheld by monarchs, such as the Tudors and the Stuarts in England; the Roman Church, which received "the cooperation of the state in controlling expression";[6] and the political philosophy and teachings of Plato. The last was carried through by Machiavelli, Thomas Hobbes, and Georg Hegel.

When authoritarian governments realized that print could disseminate information to numerous people, they controlled who could print what by requiring printers to secure licenses; they used censorship; and they punished those who printed controversial information without permission.[7] Consequently, the press was used by governments to promote continuity and harmony.[8]

There were exceptions, however. For example, certain political systems could be discussed, even criticized, in general terms, but criticism of those who wielded power was not permitted. In essence, whatever was published could not criticize the state or its citizens. Rather, it had to promote the state's political system and agenda.[9]

Richard Davis claimed that "most nations follow the authoritarian model," noting that William Rugh has identified three types of authoritarian systems: a *mobilization* press, where the press is used as a tool in the development of the nation; a *loyalist* press, which exists to provide fealty to the state rather than as a change agent; and a *diverse* press, where some degree of pluralism is tolerated and government control is more limited.[10]

Soviet-Totalitarianism

This theory of the press, although it is not the second theory chronologically speaking, is presented here because its philosophy, which is based on the ideas of Karl Marx, Vladimir Lenin, and Joseph Stalin, reminds one of authoritarianism. Indeed, as Schramm pointed out in the *Four Theories of the Press*, "From the beginning, the Marxist tradition has displayed authoritarianism."[11]

Of course, one has to realize that Marx did not devote himself to the problem of the press; the problem that concerned him was communism and how to get it accepted. But if his philosophy was accepted and adopted, the press would be used as an instrument to interpret Communist doctrine, not to criticize the government or serve as a forum for open discussion.[12] Thus, the major characteristic of Soviet-totalitarianism is similar to that of authoritarianism; that is, the press is used by those wielding power.

Since Marx's ideas were largely accepted and adapted by Lenin, then by Stalin, Marx's view of the press came true. Indeed, the media were used by the government to control and mold society. As Schramm noted, the media in the former Soviet Union reflected the "Soviet official ideology, the Soviet state, and the Soviet ideal personality."[13]

The major characteristic of Soviet-totalitarianism is that the media were used to spread the "word"—the "word" according to the Kremlin. This reminds one of authoritarian control over the press.

However, it should be noted that in Article 125 of the Constitution of the former Soviet Union, freedom of speech, freedom of the press, freedom of assembly, and freedom of strict processions and demonstrations were guaranteed. Of course, as Schramm mentioned, absolute freedom was impossible, at least from the Soviet perspective.[14] Thus, whatever was intended for the media had to be approved by an official of the state. Therefore, political philosophy dictated how the media, and in particular the press, were used. It should be noted that the former Soviet-totalitarianism system allowed the press to criticize leaders.

There are differences between the totalitarianism of the former Soviet Union and the authoritarianism of the British Isles. For example, in the Soviet system the media were state owned; in the authoritarian system the media were for the most part privately owned. Another difference is that in the Soviet system, publishing and broadcasting were state funded, not supported by advertisers. Another difference is that in the Soviet system the function of mass communications had been defined positively; authoritarianism defined it negatively. A fourth difference is that in the Soviet system mass communications was used to bring about change. In the authoritarian system mass communications was controlled to maintain the status quo. A fifth difference is that the Soviet system was based on "class warfare, and aimed at the dominance of one class, and ultimately at a classless society."[15] Authoritarianism "was based on a strict class system which was intended to persist, with lower classes paying desired service to the ruling class."[16] A final difference is that in the Soviet system mass communications was a planned system; in authoritarianism it was a controlled system.

Libertarianism

This theory developed as a result of man's interest in science, which revolutionized his way of thinking; the Reformation, which challenged the Roman Church; the growth of capitalism; and political unrest.[17] The Enlightenment of the seventeenth and eighteenth centuries helped seal its development. As Christians, Ferre, and Fackler wrote, "The Enlightenment contributed immeasurably to the acceptance and diffusion of the classical liberal self."[18]

According to Rivers, Schramm, and Christians, "the intellectual revolution was chiefly secular, not only because it challenged the authority of the one Church, but also because it tended to transfer the rewards for good conduct nearer to the arena of worldly gains."[19]

The people primarily responsible for this theory were Descartes, who emphasized reason; John Locke, who believed that people should rule; John

Milton, who wrote about a free press in *Areopagitica*; Thomas Paine, who wrote *Common Sense*; Thomas Jefferson, who spoke for a free press; and John Stuart Mill, who wrote *On Liberty*.[20]

The basic elements of libertarianism include reason, a free marketplace of ideas, and a press that checks on the government.

Theodore L. Glasser wrote, "Libertarianism begins and ends with the pre-eminence of individual liberty. It embraces liberty as the ultimate political value, a fundamentally natural and thus inalienable right of the individual to deny claims of obligation or authority."[21]

Akhavan-Majid and Wolf wrote, "Libertarianism . . . views human beings as rational and capable of discovering the truth if allowed to participate in a free marketplace of ideas."[22]

The differences between libertarianism and authoritarianism and even Soviet-totalitarianism are obvious. As mentioned, the latter two theories see man as a creature that needs help from the state. In the former, man is seen as a creature that can think things out and rationalize; man does not need the state to care for him. The state exists solely to ensure man's happiness.

Unfortunately, this press theory is being threatened because of costs. Newspapers and broadcast stations are expensive to operate; fewer are owned by competing companies. Thus, the marketplace of ideas is closing, not opening.

Social Responsibility

This theory developed in the twentieth century primarily as a result of the report by the Commission on Freedom of the Press. Critical of the media, the commission questioned the performance of the press and issued a warning that if the owners of the media continued to engage in practices that society questioned, the media would eventually be controlled or regulated by an arm of government or a committee founded for that purpose. According to Denis McQuail, "The 'theory of social responsibility' involved a view of media ownership as a form of public trust or stewardship, rather than as an unlimited private franchise."[23]

Daniel C. Hallin pointed out several factors that sparked the commission and the social responsibility theory:

> By the end of the Second World War the inadequacies of the libertarian model were evident. It was clear, first of all, that the owners of the news media were not representative of the public at large, and that democracy—and, more narrowly, the credibility and morale of news organizations themselves—was at risk if the owners had the power to use the media at will as instruments of class or personal interests. Second, it was clear that what worked to sell cultural com-

modities didn't necessarily coincide with the interest of society in substantial and accurate reporting on public affairs. And third, it had become clear that propaganda—in Habermas' terms, the use of communication as an instrument of power and profit rather than as a medium of dialogue—had become pervasive in the private sphere as well as in political life, and also threatened to undermine the market-place in ideas.[24]

The differences between this theory and libertarianism, authoritarianism, and Soviet-totalitarianism include: it can be defined by journalists, but it is not enforced; it is viewed differently by journalists; it exists in a pluralistic society, not a monolithic society (like the former Soviet Union); it expects the media to report the truth with attribution (libertarianism allows the press to distort the truth and to lie); and it emphasizes the public's right to know (libertarianism emphasizes the public's right to know according to what the publisher wants the public to know).[25]

Though libertarianism allows one to criticize the system and/or its leaders, the social responsibility theory allows one to criticize the system, its leaders, and even others within the system. To say that the social responsibility theory allows one to keep tabs on the government would not be an exaggeration. As Carl Hausman wrote, "The social responsibility theory in its basic form seems a quite reasonable reaction to the threat of excesses by the news media, and by extension can live in peaceful coexistence with the traditional libertarian theories that underlie American society."[26]

COMMENTS ON THE OPERATIONS OF THE U.S. MEDIA

Authoritarianism/Soviet-Totalitarianism

Because these theories are similar, liberty has been taken to comment on both. However, in each comment the respective theory has been identified.

These theories do not apply in the strictest sense to the U.S. press, but incidents have happened (and will continue to happen) that resemble certain aspects of both theories. For example, Hillier Krieghbaum, in *Pressure on the Press*, wrote, "Particularly biased publishers and editors have deleted any mention of individuals or groups with whom they had personal vendetta—in effect, treating these non-persons as if they had departed from the globe when the feud began."[27]

Not only is this an example of authoritarianism, but of Soviet-totalitarianism. However, there are more examples that prove that the press in the United States may be labeled authoritarian. Monopoly, for instance, is another. Ben Bagdikian, in *The Effete Conspiracy*, pointed out that the old monopoly—domination of one city by one newspaper management—is just about complete.

"The new monopoly" is that of "groups." A group, or chain, consists of a single management that controls papers in more than one city. They are growing like wildfire. Ten years ago chains controlled 491 papers, or a third of all dailies. Today a majority of the . . . dailies are operated by chains.[28]

The last sentence perhaps is the most important point made by Bagdikian, for such a monopoly encourages practitioners within these chains to rely on others' work. Thus, the one voice problem develops. Also, the company owning these newspapers may encourage the editors and reporters to slant whatever is published. Of course, how a story is slanted depends on the company's philosophy at the time.

What happens when a company or conglomerate owns more than one newspaper and television or radio station? In his article, "How Cross-Ownership Effects News-Gathering," William Gormley, Jr. claimed that when a company owned a newspaper and a television station in the same city "the variety of news available to the public was restricted."[29] Furthermore, Gormley found that "news staffs were engaged in cooperative practices that might not be described as 'abuses' but which nevertheless belied assurances by owners of newspaper-television combinations that their news staffs functioned separately and independently."[30] Gormley also found that cross-ownership reduced the willingness of television stations to editorialize. Thus, to the extent that cross-ownership undermines diversity, it threatens truth and understanding.

Such examples also threaten the social responsibility theory, in the sense that the owners/operators of the media have cheated the public of its right to know.

In these cases the owners/operators of the media have become authoritarian figures. They decided what should be read or seen or heard. Of course, there are other examples, such as the case of the Federal Trade Commission against Sears, Roebuck and Company of Chicago. In the article, "The Sins of Sears Are Not News in Chicago," Michael Hirsh reported that the FTC had accused Sears of engaging in bait-and-switch selling tactics, which Sears denied. In court, however, Sears abandoned its denial and negotiated a consent order. The hearings of the case lasted eleven days. Since it had all the ingredients of a good story, especially when employees testified that Sears had used deceptive practices on the buying public, one would have expected day-by-day coverage. But this was not the case. The *Chicago Tribune* did not publish a story until a week after the trial was halted at Sears's request. Hirsh pointed out that Sears was the newspaper's largest advertiser, spending more than $5 million annually. The *Chicago Sun-Times* published only three stories. The *Chicago Daily*

News published only two stories. There was no television coverage, and very little radio coverage.[31]

The public's right to know did not seem to matter in this case. Again, suppression of a newsworthy event occurred. Whether it was Sears's advertising in the *Chicago Tribune* or other newspapers that caused the story not to be reported is anyone's guess. However, newspapers, as well as other media, need advertising revenue to operate. This realization was undoubtedly taken into consideration. After all, reporters have very little input about what goes into a newspaper. (The same holds true for the authoritarian/Soviet-totalitarian press. In this sense, the authoritarian/Soviet-totalitarian and libertarian and social responsibility theories are similar.)

Libertarianism

Some practices of the press in the United States cause it to be labeled libertarian. For example, reporters have accepted favors, even gifts, from corporations and professional sports teams. They have accepted free trips from motel chains, hotel chains, travel agencies, and airline companies. The press has been guilty of providing editorial "plugs" to specific advertisers. The press has also been guilty of intruding into questionable territory. For instance, reporters shove microphones and cameras into faces of people who have experienced some terrible tragedy or ordeal. Of course, these reporters believe that their readers or listeners or viewers have a right to know.

In each of these examples, elements of libertarianism are evident. In other words, editors have allowed, even encouraged, their reporters to do anything, even accept bribes, to get a story.

Another incident of note is the Supreme Court's review of the press's role in the Sam Sheppard murder case. According to Hillier Krieghbaum,

> the majority court opinion cited publication of much material "never heard from the witness stand," some of which undoubtedly reached at least some of the jurors, including "a front-page picture of Mrs. Sheppard's blood-stained pillow [which] was published after being 'doctored' to show more clearly an alleged imprint of a surgical instrument," and repeated front-page headlines such as "Quit Stalling—Bring Him In," "Why Isn't Sam Sheppard in Jail?" and "But Who Will Speak for Marilyn?"[32]

In this instance, the press was acting like a mob; that is, it wanted a suspect to harass and then hang. The fact that a person has a right to a fair trial apparently did not matter to the reporters and photographers assigned to cover the story.

Why has the press repeatedly attacked the "little guy"? The reason is simple. Besides keeping the status quo, the press publishes only what is given to it. In other words, little significant information is given to the press by representatives of the government (local, state, federal), even if the press requests it. As Ralph Nader learned, getting information from the federal government is similar to jogging in traffic. One does not know which way to go and there is no one willing to help. In his study of the Freedom of Information Act, for example, he found specific tactics used by bureaucrats: delay, misclassification, high charges, complicated appeals, and inconsistent interpretations.[33]

Nader charged that reporters were not as aggressive as they should be. He believed that if they had wanted the information badly enough, they would have followed through to the courts on denials of agency information.

Such deceitful methods by the federal government apparently inhibit what can be reported by the press. Nonetheless, one has to agree with Nader: the information can be gotten if the press is seriously interested. According to the press, the problem is that it does not have the time and, in some cases, the money to get the information. Another reason provided by the press is that it has too few reporters. Of course, anyone who examines *The Powers That Be* by David Halberstam, *Making News* by Gaye Tuchman, *News from Nowhere* by Edward Jay Epstein, *On Press* by Tom Wicker, *Deciding What's News* by Herbert Gans, *Market-Driven Journalism: Let the Citizen Beware?* by John H. McManus, *The News About the News: American Journalism in Peril* by Leonard Downie, Jr., and Robert G. Kaiser, *News Incorporated: Corporate Media Ownership and Its Threat to Democracy* edited by Elliot D. Cohen, and other books critiquing the press will realize that the above assertions are mere excuses. It seems that the press does not go after a story; rather, a story goes after the press. For example, as one former reporter put it, most attacks on the federal government are reactions to behavior rather than prodding, seeking, investigative reporting. Nor is information of significance given to the press by big business. Today, because there are so many newspapers and broadcasting stations owned by large corporations, it is unreasonable to think that the press is going to bite the hand that feeds it.

Social Responsibility

This theory probably exists at the national level more than at the local level; that is, at the larger newspapers, television networks, and radio networks instead of at the smaller newspapers, local television stations, and local radio stations. In other words, the local media are responsible to a smaller audience; thus, what they print or air may have repercussions. The national media, since they do not have a small audience, do not have to question whether this story or that story will cause or have a specific effect or consequence, unless it causes thousands of people to complain to the national media or, worse, to the advertisers. This is not to say that these larger newspapers and networks are not responsible for their content—they are, but one living in a small town cannot very well visit an editor of the *New York Times* to complain about a story. Or, if the person complains via the Internet, the editor probably will not respond according to the person's wishes; whereas if the person reads a story not to his liking in a local newspaper, he may very well visit the editor. The point is this: The editor of a local newspaper will not, in most cases, cause his readers to dislike him. After all, he depends on them for his livelihood. If they do not subscribe to his newspaper, advertisers will not buy space. The same is true of the local radio and television stations. This may be one reason for television news to change to a less serious format. Indeed, television news, even at the network level, focuses more on packaging than on content.

Carl Sessions Stepp claims that several contemporary conditions have affected the social responsibility theory of the press. These include: "(1) intensified concentration"; "(2) the increasing intrusion of non-news corporations into the news enterprise"; "(3) the rise of broadcasting"; and "(4) a perceived economic and social squeeze on the news media."[34] The first has elevated business considerations over journalistic considerations. The second has caused the print media to become merely another profit-making entity. The third has caused the print media to place an emphasis on entertainment rather than on hard news. The fourth has made publishers of newspapers realize that their products are vulnerable. Indeed, as a result of fewer readers and subsequently fewer advertisers, several major newspapers have died in the last few years.

In his assessment of local television news, Ron Powers observed,

> Most large-city news departments offered, in addition, a noble-sounding catalog of secondary news services: consumer tips; perhaps a mini-documentary, in several parts, on some civic issues; an "action" reporter who was a conspicuous participant in the stories he or she covered; often a minority advocate, handsome/beautiful and vaguely ethnic, . . . an "ombudsman" reporter who checked out complaints against local businesses and services.[35]

Powers also claimed that when a station creates a news program according to guidelines provided by researchers, the news program is designed for gratifying the viewers' whims, not for providing detailed information. As a result, a hoax is perpetrated on the American public. Powers wrote, "The hoax is made more insidious by the fact that very few TV news-watchers are aware of what information is *left out* of a newscast to make room for the audience-building gimmicks and pleasant repartee."[36]

Of course, as Powers pointed out, such formats do entertain the viewer. But if entertainment outweighs the information, the viewer may not get the most important part of the story. In most stories, the *why* is the most important element. Yet, most television stories fail to focus on this element. Therefore, responsibility to the viewer has been overlooked. It should be mentioned that advertising rates for a television news program, like other programs, are based on ratings—that is, how many people actually watch the program. If the ratings are high, the advertising rates can be high, and vice versa. Also, stories of a controversial nature may upset someone in Congress, or someone within the Federal Communications Commission. Because stations have to get licenses from this commission to operate, they are, technically speaking, at the government's mercy—that is, to a certain extent. However, during the Reagan administration, the Federal Communications Commission was weakened by a lack of funding. When Bush became president, funding for the Federal Communications Commission was increased. Today, the commission is stronger because of funding. Unfortunately, its policy seems to be "hands off"—that is, let networks and stations do whatever they please.

What about the press—the newspapers—and social responsibility? Although newspapers such as the *New York Times* and the *Washington Post* occasionally suppress stories, the local newspaper is more apt to cut a controversial story, especially when the story concerns a local citizen or local business, or something that would upset the community. This has happened in numerous newspapers numerous times.

Ben Bagdikian, for example, pointed out,

> When civil rights became an issue, many segregationist editors censored out news of integrationist agitation, believing they were doing it for the good of the community. Other editors censored out news of segregationist-agitation, believing they were doing it for the good of the community.[37]

The larger newspapers, on the other hand, are more likely to publish information of a controversial nature—unless the information is directly related to the newspaper. Then suppression may be used.

In order for the social responsibility theory to be more than an idea, it is necessary for publishers to be more than mere business people, and it is necessary for editors and reporters to realize that their responsibility is to present factual stories—as factual as possible—to their readers. Only when this happens can this theory transform into actuality.

ADDENDUM

In 1971, in *Media, Messages, and Men*, Ralph Lowenstein retained "Authoritarianism" and "Libertarianism," but he changed "Soviet-totalitarianism" to "Social Centralist," which was a broader concept. Indeed, "Social Centralist" conveyed the collectivist orientation and the centrally guided nature of the press in the Communist countries. He changed "Social Responsibility" to "Social Libertarian," primarily to emphasize the relationship between the "Social Responsibility" and "Libertarian" concepts and to suggest "that some regulation of the media may be required to ensure public benefit" (Whitney R. Mundt, "Global Media Philosophies," *Global Journalism: Survey of International Communication*, ed. John C. Merrill [New York: Longman Publishing Group, 1991], 17). Eight years later, Lowenstein changed "Social Centralist" to "Social Authoritarian" to emphasize the authoritarian roots of government-press relations in Communist countries (Roya Akhavan-Majid and Gary Wolf, "American Mass Media and the Myth of Libertarianism: Toward an 'Elite Power Group' Theory," *Critical Studies in Mass Communication* [June 1991], 140). He applied "Social Centralist" to the systems that allowed governments to interact with the press "to assure the operational spirit of the libertarian philosophy" (Mundt 1991, 18).

In 1974, in *The Imperative of Freedom*, John Merrill argued that a philosophy of the press could not be both libertarian (free) and directed (controlled). Merrill proposed a "Political Press Circle" that put "Libertarianism" at the top and "Authoritarianism" at the bottom of a circle. Thus, he reduced the four theories of the press to two. He put "Socialism" on the left-hand side of the circle and "Capitalism" on the right-hand side. Thus, the path from freedom to statism proceeded in either direction; left, socialism, or right, capitalism (Mundt 1991, 18).

In 1981, in *The World News Prism*, William Hachten proposed the following typology: "Authoritarian"; "Communist"; "Western," which included Libertarianism and Social Responsibility; "Revolutionary"; and "Developmental." Of course, "Communist" was the same as "Soviet-totalitarianism." The models "Revolutionary" and "Developmental" referred to those who used the press to overthrow the current government and to governments that used the press to achieve integration and development, respectively (Akhavan-Majid and Wolf 1991, 141).

In 1983, in *Mass Communication Theory: An Introduction*, Denis McQuail replaced "Libertarianism" with "Free Press Theory," which basically meant the same. He also discussed "Development Media Theory," which applied to the press in developing countries, and "Democratic-participant Media Theory," which "lies with the needs, interests and aspirations of the 'receiver' in a political society. It has to do with the right to relevant information, the right to answer back, the right to use the means of communication for interaction in small scale settings of community, interest group, and subculture. The theory rejects the necessity of uniform, centralized, high cost, highly professionalized, state-controlled media. It favors multiplicity, smallness of scale, locality, deinstitutionalization, interchange of sender-receiver roles, horizontality of communication links at all levels of society, interaction" (Denis McQuail, *Mass Communication Theory: An Introduction* [London: SAGE Publications, Ltd., 1983], 97).

J. Herbert Altschull, in *Agents of Power*, published in 1984, chose "modified economic identifications" relating to the political designations of First, Second, and Third World. The First, or Western World, became the "Market" movement. The Second, or Eastern World, became the "Marxist" movement. The Third, or Southern World, became the "Advancing" movement. Market journalists, according to Altschull, served the people and concurrently promoted capitalism. These journalists served as watchdogs of the government. Marxist journalists served the people by promoting socialism. These journalists presented specific views primarily to change behavior. Advancing journalists served the people and the government by promoting change. These journalists served as tools of peace. The press in the Market movement was not manipulated by power. The press in the Marxist movement countered oppression. The press in the Advancing movement was not as important as the visibility of the nation (Mundt 1991, 22).

In 1985, in *The Press and the Decline of Democracy*, Robert Picard placed "Democratic Socialist" beside "Social Responsibility" and "Libertarianism" in Hachten's Western theory of the press. According to Picard, "Democratic Socialist," like the "Social Responsibility" theory, stipulated that journalists have to "open avenues for the expression of diverse ideas and opinions" (Picard 1985, 67). Picard also claimed that this model advocated "state action to institute new forms of ownership, operation, and management of the media and significant state intervention in the economics of the press" (Picard 1985, 67). Of course, this model was in response to the growing concentration of press ownership, which Picard criticized.

Also in 1985, in *World Broadcasting Systems*, Sydney Head addressed government-media relationships in broadcasting. According to Head, broadcasters in the United States enjoyed a free enterprise system, while broadcasters in England were controlled by a public corporation. Broadcasters in the former Soviet Union were controlled by the government. Head claimed that the system in the United States was *permissive*, while the system in England was *paternalistic.* The system in the former Soviet Union was *authoritarian* (Mundt 1991, 26–27).

In 1991, Akhavan-Majid and Wolf proposed the "Elite Power Group" model, which was in response to several conditions affecting the press in America: concentration of ownership, integration with other power elites, and two-way flow of influence (government influence on the mass media and vice versa). This model, according to the authors, was more accurate in its description of the press in America than "Libertarianism" (Akhavan-Majid and Wolf 1991, 139–51).

In 2005, in the fifth edition of *McQuail's Mass Communication Theory,* Denis McQuail presented four models pertaining to normative media theory: a liberal-pluralist or market model, which is based on the libertarian theory; a social responsibility or public interest model, which is based on the social responsibility theory; a professional model; and an alternative media model. The professional model is based on the idea that "the guardianship of standards belong in the model to the 'press' itself and to the journalistic profession." The alternative media model "represents a range of non-mainstream media, with different aims and origins. . . . It emphasizes the rights of subcultures with their particularistic values and promotes intersubjective understanding and a real sense of community" (McQuail 2005, 185–86).

In 2009, Clifford G. Christians, Theodore L. Glasser, Denis McQuail, Kaarle Nordenstreng, and Robert A. White wrote *Normative Theories of the Media: Journalism in Democratic Societies.* Christians et al. claimed that freedom of the press depended on the economic, political, and social environment in which the media operated. The authors identified four roles for the media—monitorial, facilitative, radical, and collaborative—in westernized societies. The first, monitorial, applies when reporters act as observers and report objectively about their subjects. The second, facilitative, applies when the media provide a platform so citizens can express themselves. In essence, the media supports or strengthens society. The third, radical, applies when the media confronts or opposes the prevailing power structure. The media can call for revolution. The fourth, collaborative, applies when the media collaborates with the prevailing power structure, primarily to advance mutually acceptable interests.

NOTES

1. William L. Rivers, Wilbur Schramm, and Clifford G. Christians, *Responsibility in Mass Communication* (New York: Harper and Row, 1980), 31.

2. Rivers, Schramm, and Christians, *Responsibility in Mass Communication,* 32.

3. Rivers, Schramm, and Christians, *Responsibility in Mass Communication,* 32.

4. Roya Akhavan-Majid and Gary Wolf, "American Mass Media and the Myth of Libertarianism: Toward an 'Elite Power Group' Theory," *Critical Studies in Mass Communication* 8 (1991), 140.

5. Denis McQuail, *McQuail's Mass Communication Theory*, 5th ed. (London: SAGE Publications Ltd., 2005), 176.

6. Rivers, Schramm, and Christians, *Responsibility in Mass Communication*, 32–33.

7. Rivers, Schramm, and Christians, *Responsibility in Mass Communication*, 33–34.

8. Rivers, Schramm, and Christians, *Responsibility in Mass Communication*, 34.

9. Rivers, Schramm, and Christians, *Responsibility in Mass Communication*, 35.

10. Richard Davis, *The Press and American Politics: The New Mediator* (White Plains, N.Y.: Longman Publishing Group, 1992), 131.

11. Fred S. Siebert, Theodore Peterson, and Wilbur Schramm, *Four Theories of the Press* (Freeport, N.Y.: Books for Libraries Press, 1973), 107.

12. Siebert, Peterson, and Schramm, *Four Theories of the Press*, 110.

13. Siebert, Peterson, and Schramm, *Four Theories of the Press*, 116.

14. Siebert, Peterson, and Schramm, *Four Theories of the Press*, 126.

15. Siebert, Peterson, and Schramm, *Four Theories of the Press*, 141.

16. Siebert, Peterson, and Schramm, *Four Theories of the Press*, 141.

17. Rivers, Schramm, and Christians, *Responsibility in Mass Communication*, 38.

18. Clifford G. Christians, John P. Ferre, and P. Mark Fackler, *Good News: Social Ethics and the Press* (New York: Oxford University Press, 1993), 26.

19. Rivers, Schramm, and Christians, *Responsibility in Mass Communication*, 39.

20. Rivers, Schramm, and Christians, *Responsibility in Mass Communication*, 40–41.

21. Theodore L. Glasser, "Press Responsibility and First Amendment Values," *Responsible Journalism*, edited by Deni Elliott (Beverly Hills, Calif.: SAGE Publications, 1986), 82.

22. Akhavan-Majid and Wolf, "American Mass Media and the Myth of Libertarianism," 140.

23. McQuail, *McQuail's Mass Communication Theory*, 171.

24. Daniel C. Hallin, *We Keep America on Top of the World: Television Journalism and the Public Sphere* (New York: Routledge, 1994), 3–4.

25. Rivers, Schramm, and Christians, *Responsibility in Mass Communication*, 47–48.

26. Carl Hausman, *Crisis of Conscience: Perspectives on Journalism Ethics* (New York: HarperCollins, 1992), 46.

27. Hillier Krieghbaum, *Pressures on the Press* (New York: Harper and Row, 1972), 11.

28. Ben Bagdikian, *The Effete Conspiracy* (New York: Harper and Row, 1972), 11.

29. William Gormley, Jr., "How Cross-Ownership Effects News-Gathering," *Columbia Journalism Review* (May/June 1977), 38.

30. Gormley, Jr., "How Cross-Ownership Effects News-Gathering," 39.

31. Michael Hirsh, "The Sins of Sears Are Not News in Chicago," *Columbia Journalism Review* (July/August 1976), 29–30.

32. Krieghbaum, *Pressures on the Press,* 15.

33. Krieghbaum, *Pressures on the Press,* 56.

34. Carl Sessions Stepp, "Access in a Post-Social Responsibility Age," *Democracy and the Mass Media,* edited by Judith Lichtenberg (Cambridge, England: Cambridge University Press, 1990), 189–93.

35. Ron Powers, "Eyewitless News," *Columbia Journalism Review* (May/June 1977), 18.

36. Powers, "Eyewitless News," 23.

37. Ben Bagdikian, "The Gentle Suppression," *Columbia Journalism Review* (Spring 1965), 17.

Freedom of the Press

This chapter provides reasons supported by evidence for the author's contention that the most basic responsibility of the mass media in the United States is to remain free and points out problems created by the press that threaten its freedom.

THE FIRST AMENDMENT AND ITS HISTORY

Prelude

Freedom of the press undoubtedly is one of the most important freedoms in a democratic society. Although influences or threats, such as business, advertising, and specific organized groups, among others, exist, the biggest influence or threat unquestionably is the government. Media actions that contribute to heightening this particular form of threat will be examined exclusively.

The History of the First Amendment

This amendment was not the most important item on the agenda when the fifty-five founding fathers drew up the U.S. Constitution in 1787. In fact, when James Madison's journal of the secret proceedings was published fifty-three years later, it revealed only one reference to press freedom—a motion by delegates from Massachusetts and South Carolina "that the liberty of the press should be inviolably observed."[1]

As Michael Emery pointed out, the majority of the delegates believed that the power of the Congress did not extend to the press. Consequently, the motion died.[2]

When the framers of the U.S. Constitution finished their document there was no Bill of Rights. When state conventions met to ratify the U.S. Constitution they asked that amendments be added so that power would not be abused. The state of Virginia had a Declaration of Rights from which twelve amendments were proposed. Eventually ten were submitted to the states for ratification. These ten became the Bill of Rights.

As Emery mentioned, "The press freedom clause went through various forms, some of which would have applied to the states, or to all branches of government, not just Congress."[3]

The First Amendment, which had been worked out by Madison and others in a House-Senate conference committee, provided:

> Congress shall make no law respecting an establishment of religion, or prohibiting the free exercise thereof; or abridging the freedom of speech, or of the press, or the right of the people peaceably to assemble, and to petition the government for a redress of grievance.

Thomas I. Emerson, in "The State of the First Amendment as We Enter '1984,'" claimed that the purpose of the First Amendment "was to support the principles of an open and self-governing society."[4] He added, "More specifically, it was intended to protect speakers who criticized the government, to forbid censorship of the press, and to permit assemblies in the public halls or demonstrations on the street."[5]

But how free was the press?

Within nine years after the ratification of the Bill of Rights, freedom of the press became a question rather than a statement of fact. With the passage of the Alien and Sedition Acts in 1798, it was a federal offense to "write, utter or publish . . . any false, scandalous or malicious writing . . . against the government of the United States, or either house of Congress . . . or the President."[6]

Judith Schenck Koffler, in "The New Seditious Libel," wrote, "Seditious libel is the crime of criticizing the government. It transforms dissent, which the First Amendment has traditionally been thought to protect, into heresy."[7] The Alien and Sedition Acts did not include the vice president, who was Thomas Jefferson, the political opponent of President Adams. Thus, pro-French, pro-Jefferson editors were "fair game."

Fortunately, the sedition law died in 1801 and remained dead until World War I. Nonetheless, it had been applied, even to the press, and as a result "awakened many persons to the freedom issues involved."[8]

The press saw other crises, however. During the 1830s, mobs condemned abolitionist editors, killing Elijah Lovejoy in 1837. Over the next two decades several states passed laws prohibiting anyone from subscribing to newspapers opposed to slavery.[9]

The Civil War presented another crisis. News reports, especially those sent by telegraph, were first checked by Secretary of War Edwin Stanton's office personnel. Then sometimes these were delayed or stopped.[10]

During World War I the Espionage and Sedition Acts were passed, and about one hundred newspapers were banned from the mails.[11]

In 1919–1920, the "Red Scare" caused journalists to be accused of being communistic if they did not speak against the Bolshevik Revolution in Russia or the Industrial Workers of the World (IWW) movement in America. Similarly, in the early 1950s, journalists were accused of being soft on communism or "pink" if they attacked Senator Joseph McCarthy and his "Red Scare."[12]

The 1960s and early 1970s presented another crisis for the press. The Vietnam War, which was supported by the press in the early years partly because it was pressured into accepting the administration's interpretation of the conflict, helped ignite a battle over press freedom. In 1971, in the Pentagon Papers case, for the first time in American history, the government encouraged the courts to impose prior restraint; consequently, four newspapers were ordered to halt publication concerning the Pentagon Papers. Later, the order was lifted.

The press was not alone. The broadcasting industry was attacked, too, especially by the Nixon administration. For instance, Frank Stanton, president of CBS, refused to release certain materials used in making the documentary, "The Selling of the Pentagon," and was subsequently threatened with contempt of Congress.[13]

Former Vice President Agnew made vigorous attacks on the fairness of the press. These attacks were used by former President Nixon on October 26, 1973, as the Watergate scandal was discrediting him and his White House staff. After he charged the media of distorted reporting, Patrick Buchanan, his aide, pressed for legal action to break the power of ABC, CBS, and NBC.[14]

Even the dean of broadcasters, Walter Cronkite, was criticized for his role in reporting Watergate.

Although other presidential administrations complained about the press, President Reagan's administration eliminated the press from the military invasion of Grenada. When Bill Clinton was president, the press was criticized for its reliance on unidentified sources, its investigative leaks, and its emphasis on Clinton's sex scandals. President Bush's administration criticized the press for its coverage of the War on Terrorism, although some of the press cooperated with the administration by not publishing or broadcasting certain stories whenever the stories were considered questionable or possibly causing additional acts of terrorism.

GOVERNMENT CONTROLS

Jackie Harrison, in *News*, wrote,

> Freedom of expression implies the right of criticism of governments and other
> agencies which seek to control or influence society (such as political parties,
> large corporations or commercial interests), and the interrogation and explora-
> tion of new cultural ideas and views which challenge and develop established
> norms and values. News is of course inevitably implicated in such a right, and
> the accurate (and sincere) reporting of contemporary events requires freedom
> of expression.[15]

Years earlier Wilson Dizard, Jr., wrote, "The First Amendment's prohibi-
tions against political interference with media remain a formidable barrier
against direct government intervention. It is, however, by no means a guaran-
tor against more indirect kinds of interference."[16] Dizard realized that the First
Amendment played an important role in the United States, but that it did not
necessarily protect the press in every instance.

Even though the First Amendment guarantees freedom of the press, one
must realize that freedom is never absolute. As pointed out, freedom of the
press has had limitations and stipulations attached to it.

However, as John L. Hulteng and Roy Paul Nelson mentioned, "the liberties
and freedoms of a people weaken and die when access is cut off to a continuing
flow of honest and uncensored news about what is happening in the state, the
nation, and the world."[17]

Rulers of countries know this; in order to establish an authoritarian or to-
talitarian society, the media are usually controlled first.

> Once the press is under control, the people no longer are exposed to anything
> other than the doctored propaganda the state permits them to read or hear. . . .
> The media of information thus constitute the jugular vein of a democracy; strike
> there decisively and the wound is mortal.
>
> The importance of the information media to the survival of democratic free-
> doms stems from the basic concept of a representative system of government:
> if the people are fully and accurately informed, they will be able to choose their
> governors wisely.[18]

Freedom of the press is important in a democratic society. But what does
freedom of the press mean? Unfortunately, Supreme Court justices have not
come up with a definitive answer. For example, Hugo L. Black and William
O. Douglas argued that the First Amendment meant exactly what it said, that
it was absolute, subject to no restrictions.[19] However, Chief Justice Burger

insisted that the Supreme Court had not provided the press with special privilege. He claimed that the framers of the U.S. Constitution had merely added the clause regarding the press so that written speech would be protected along with oral speech.[20] Thus, one can understand why freedom of the press has suffered from infractions. If the Supreme Court justices cannot decide on what the founding fathers meant, who can?

Censorship

Printed media have been banned by the United States Postal Service more than once. As mentioned, numerous newspapers were banned during World War I. Books and magazines have been banned, too. In 1978, for example, the Postal Service won eleven convictions against pornographic material.[21]

Paul Gilbert claimed that censorship should not play a major role in democratic societies. He wrote, "In democratic societies the only area in which it is openly accepted that censorship has a part to play is in the field of military security."[22]

Nonetheless, even the film industry, which has a movie rating system, has been censored, more by states and municipalities than by the federal government, especially in cases involving indecency. But the industry as a whole has tested obscenity restrictions by producing more movies of a questionable nature. Even so-called hard-core films have flooded the market; some, such as *Deep Throat* and *Anyone but My Husband*, have been removed from theaters, however.[23]

Radio and television broadcasting, since both are under the continuing regulation of the Federal Communications Commission (FCC), have seen frequent attacks and threats of censorship. However, since the early 1980s, when the National Association of Broadcasters Radio Code and the National Association of Broadcasters Television Code were cancelled and when the FCC's budget was dramatically curtailed by the Reagan administration, broadcasters, especially the major networks, have enjoyed more freedom, particularly in regard to their programming. Nonetheless, local stations are supposed to operate in the public interest and meet community needs in order to have their licenses renewed. Thus, both radio and television stations are limited in what can be broadcast.

Libel

The First Amendment, according to the courts, "does not render the publisher immune from responsibility *after the fact* of publication, if what he has published injures other well-established and safeguarded rights."[24]

Although there is no such thing as a federal law of libel, all of the fifty states have statutes that define it: a publication that damages the reputation of an individual or group of individuals. Donna A. Demac wrote, "Libel is defined as communication—words or pictures—that tends to expose someone to public ridicule, shame, or contempt, or otherwise damages a person's reputation."[25]

In the first definition, the term of *publication* embraces not only the print media, but radio and television broadcasting. Therefore, the media as a whole may, in certain circumstances, be accountable.

As Demac wrote,

> Television newscasts, editorials, history books, biographies, and even novels and cartoons have been subjected to libel suits brought by public officials, celebrities, and others who find themselves depicted in ways that displease them. Suits against student publications are also on the rise.[26]

There have been several developments, however, which have made the media more vulnerable to libel suits and have made the libel suits more damaging. According to Eve Pell,

> Among these developments are increases in the number of libel suits filed, sky-high legal expenses, the risk of losing hundreds of thousands or millions of dollars in damage verdicts, a more hostile attitude toward the press in the courts, particularly on the part of juries, and a strong public perception that the press is not fair and ought to be made so.[27]

According to Pell, punitive damages have been the major problem for the news media. She wrote, "No insurance can be purchased that is guaranteed to cover these damages; several states have laws stating that punitive damages cannot be paid by insurance, and in those states insurance companies have refused to pay punitive awards."[28]

Also, as Demac pointed out, even when libel suits are decided in favor of the defendants, the energy and expense involved to prepare a defense has a chilling effect on future coverage.[29] Alan U. Schwartz, in "Using the Courts to Muzzle the Press," expressed a similar notion:

> Publishers and broadcasters of all kinds are now coming to realize that the cost of defending libel and privacy suits—and the uncertainty of result because of unclear guidelines—adds another link of self-censorship to the claim which can eventually strangle free expression through governmental intimidation rather than action.[30]

Nonetheless, these statutes also explain ways by which publishers or broadcasters can defend themselves against libel suits. This is not to say that publishers or broadcasters will escape damages sought by readers or viewers, however. If the publication or broadcasting station has published or aired something false about a person and knows that it is false, the libel plaintiff will probably win.

Privacy

According to Andrew Belsey, there are three types of privacy: "(1) bodily or physical privacy"; "(2) mental or communicational privacy"; and "(3) informational privacy."[31] The first refers to space in which one functions, the second refers to one's being left alone to think, and the third refers to personal information that is legitimately placed in files and folders within organizations and other entities. The press is not mentioned in any of Belsey's definitions. Yet, occasionally, certain individuals may find themselves thrust into the public eye involuntarily. When this occurs, the press is usually present and will in all likelihood write about and even record the individuals, even if they wish otherwise. Consent is not necessarily requested by the press in such instances.

Arthur R. Miller, in "Overzealous Reporters vs. the Right to Privacy," wrote,

> Unless reporters are deterred from excessive and unwarranted curiosity, many of us may be inhibited from participating in society's affairs. Any risk of dampening press enthusiasm for newsgathering must be measured against creating a public fear, what George Orwell called "the assumption that every sound you made was overheard, and, except in darkness, every move was scrutinized."[32]

Nonetheless, this right is questionable when the person becomes news. For example, public officials have little claim to privacy. Similarly, movie stars, rock stars, television personalities, and such have lesser claim to privacy than average citizens.

Free Press versus Fair Trial

Without question, the First Amendment, which guarantees a free press, seems to be at odds with the Sixth Amendment, which guarantees the accused a fair trial by an impartial jury. In other words, can the accused receive a fair trial when the press reports and comments on the crime?

Clifton Daniel, in "Fair Trial and Freedom of the Press," claimed that the press sometimes does "violence to the rights of defendants," and that the manners of news personnel "are not always impeccable." Further, "the press sometimes swarms over a news story in such a way that the story becomes warped and distorted." Daniel stated that reporters believe reform is needed and that reporters "must be more conscientious" in their concern "for the rights of individuals."[33]

Louis Nizer made this point much stronger in "Trial by Headline." He wrote,

> Frequently, those who defined the present practice of the press speak of its "right to know." There is no such right. The press has "the right to publish." No citizen owes the duty to the press to inform it about his or her personal life. No district attorney need report the progress of an investigation. No lawyer must confide his trial plans.[34]

Nizer added that a public trial was for the benefit of the defendant, not for the press. "Attendance of the public prevents the courts from becoming instruments of persecution."[35]

Indeed, as a result of what happened at the Bruno Hauptmann trial, the American Bar Association in 1937 passed Canon 35, which sought to ban radio from the courtroom. (Hauptmann had been accused of kidnapping and murdering the Lindbergh child. His trial attracted more reporters than any other murder trial had up to that time. Hauptmann was found guilty and sentenced to death.) Television had become popular by 1952. As a result, it, too, was banned by Canon 35.[36] It should be mentioned that the press was not alone in trying Hauptmann. The attorneys as well as the police spoke freely to reporters about the case, as did the defendant.

Another trial by the press instead of the jury was of Dr. Samuel Sheppard. Like the Hauptmann case, this one had all the elements of interest: Dr. Sheppard was young and handsome, an osteopath who was accused of murdering his beautiful wife. The media played up the family's prominence, the other woman, and the other man who was supposed to have been in the house.[37]

As in the Hauptmann case, reporters and photographers from all over the United States were present. Again, information was leaked by both the prosecution and the defense teams to members of the press, and certain experts not only discussed the evidence but added evidence in their talks with members of the press.

The jury found Dr. Sheppard guilty, and the judge sentenced him to life in prison. After ten years, in 1966, he was released. The U.S. Supreme Court ruled that the "carnival atmosphere" of the trial had deprived Dr. Sheppard of his constitutional rights.[38]

As a result of these and similar cases, court proceedings have been supervised by strict, discretionary judges. In 1968, the American Bar Association suggested that a trial should be closed to the media at various stages primarily as a means of preventing excesses.[39] And some states have allowed judges to institute gag orders, which prohibit the media from trials.

In recent years, however, state governments and judges have allowed not only reporters but TV cameras into courtrooms. Indeed, in the case of O. J. Simpson, the prosecution and defense teams seemed to cater to representatives of the media throughout the trial, and specific witnesses, as some legal authorities have speculated, perhaps dressed and responded to questions in a certain way as a result of knowing that they would be sitting in front of a camera. If this is true, how much of an effect did this have on the jury's verdict?

On the other hand, newsmen, to a great extent, have agreed "that there have been some spectacular abuses of news coverage of criminal cases; they will not attempt to defend such excesses."[40] And these excesses, it must be remembered, invite and lead to loss of freedom. In short, freedom is weakened when a breakdown in responsibility occurs.

However, as Hulteng and Nelson pointed out, editors dislike the approach suggested by the American Bar Association. Indeed, editors claim that the public needs to learn how justice operates at every stage, not just the first or last stage, particularly in high-profile cases.[41]

But journalists have to remember that all judges have the power to cite and punish for contempt. And this includes outbursts in the courtroom and statements made orally or in print.

Government Secrecy

The founders who wrote the U.S. Constitution met in secrecy to discuss what should be in the document. Consequently, is it little wonder that today's politicians meet in secrecy? Is it little wonder that classified information is withheld from the media?

The founders of the United States withheld information—perhaps important information—from the public. Although most believed in the freedom of the press, hypocrisy filled the first assembly because the press was not present. When Washington became the first president, he established the doctrine of executive privilege, which has been relied upon by most, if not all, presidents since to thwart specific journalists.

During the Eisenhower administration, secrecy became the "in thing." The president shielded Defense Department officials from having to testify before Joseph McCarthy. (Some would argue that President Eisenhower did what was right.) Other executive departments and agencies used this tactic to conceal information. And, although section 1002 of the Administrative Procedure Act holds that "all matters of official record" in the federal government must be made available for publication, because of three abstract exemptions it was used to conceal information.[42]

As a result, the Freedom of Information Act was signed into law by President Johnson in 1966. This bill had intended to give citizens access to all public transactions, but by the time it was enacted, nine exemptions had been attached.[43] The bill was amended in 1974 to assist the press in the information-gathering process. However, as Demac noted, numerous government agencies have taken extremely long periods of time to respond to requests and have even denied the existence of specific requested information.[44]

Although there may be times when publishers and broadcasters should be censored, especially if suppression of the information is unquestionably in the best interest of the nation, Thomas I. Emerson, in "The Danger of State Secrecy," wrote, "secrecy in government accompanies evil in government. There is, indeed, a symbiotic relationship—government wrongs are kept secret because they are evil; and evil is done because it can be kept secret."[45]

What has been the media's reaction to this secrecy? Quite negative, to say the least. Spokespersons have said that unless the information can cause harm to national security it should be given to the public so that the people may know what the government is doing. Only then can a responsible form of democracy exist. The media spokespersons have a point, to a certain extent. If the public is ill informed, then the nation will have a government that is ill (in the sense that it will not necessarily act rationally or logically, or adhere to the documents on which the country was founded). Some who work in media believe officials of the federal government acted irresponsibly toward prisoners who had been members of terrorist organizations. For instance, George W. Bush's administration was criticized by some journalists for allowing "water boarding" of prisoners. Of course, others who worked for the media did not condemn the practice in print or on the air probably because they deemed it necessary to gather information. (It is possible that some of these journalists realized that the prisoners were known terrorists. It is also possible that some of these journalists believed some of the prisoners deserved to be executed.)

As shown, there are laws and some court powers that do constitute government controls on the press. Yet, press freedom has not ceased to exist. As the early 1970s illustrated, the power of the press may be stronger than the power of the presidency.

Deregulation

The broadcast industry witnessed deregulation during the 1980s. Although the Reagan administration has been identified with deregulation, the Carter administration actually considered deregulation. Since as early as 1980, the Federal Communications Commission has accepted the notion that the government should allow the broadcast industry to operate in a free, market-driven society. Consequently, several regulations that had been applied by the Federal Communications Commission were eliminated or revised. For instance, the time devoted to commercials for advertisers had been limited to eighteen minutes per hour. The Federal Communications Commission dismissed this specific rule. Certain regulations pertaining to programming were also discarded, as all-talk broadcast stations came into existence. Even the regulation pertaining to license renewal was changed. In 1981, for instance, licenses were extended from three years to five years for television and from three years to seven years for radio. Regulations pertaining to ownership of broadcast stations were revised. Indeed, prior to August 1984, a single owner could not have more than seven AM radio stations, seven FM radio stations, and seven television stations. The number of stations in each category that a single owner could have was increased to twelve. The only stipulation was that an owner of television stations could not have more than 25 percent of the nation's viewers.[46]

Dennis W. Mazzocco claimed that deregulation of the broadcast media has "contributed to a greater separation between social classes. It has also increased the political-economic division between those who are information-rich, and those who are information-poor."[47] Mazzocco also wrote,

> There is less diversity of program choices today than there was before the FCC began to deregulate the U.S. broadcast sector in the late 1970s. . . . Also true is that many more major metropolitan newspapers are interlocked via corporate connections to other segments of electronic media ownership. The result is a national and local press that has become a lapdog to government and corporate power.[48]

MEDIA-MADE PROBLEMS: A THREAT TO FREEDOM OF THE PRESS

In the article, "First Amendment Revisionism," Ben Bagdikian warned that sins committed by the press may cause the government to revise the First Amendment. He wrote, "In the most serious legal battle to date, there is a chance that the First Amendment, as journalists have come to know it, will be altered to cover some forms of access to communications media. If that happens, the press will have only itself to blame."[49]

In addition to what has been mentioned (i.e., reporters being harassed by judges; local, state, and federal officials; celebrities; and even private citizens), reporters and the press as an institution have lost esteem. Confidence in the press is not high. Part of the reason is what Bagdikian termed "arrogance of power."

The media—especially the people who run it—have lost touch with reality. They criticize the government when they think the government is infringing on the First Amendment. Yet, when they need a favor, such as the Newspaper Preservation Act, which exempted forty-four newspapers in twenty-two cities from antitrust action and overturned a U.S. Supreme Court decision that would have dissolved a media enterprise in Tucson, they seemingly do not appreciate it. Perhaps the press is filled with cynics or frustrated hopeful novelists. Or perhaps it is filled with professional business people who care little about responsible journalism.

What is wrong with the media, specifically the press? Is it going to cause itself to be ruled or governed like radio and television? Of course, many conservatives and perhaps a few liberals probably believe that radio, television, newspapers, magazines, and even the Internet should be regulated, considering what is being broadcast or printed today. As mentioned, the public has little faith in the press. In fact, in some studies television news is believed by the public to be more accurate than newspaper news, whereas the opposite should be the case. Perhaps one of the causes of this dilemma was identified by Bagdikian when he claimed that the majority of newspapers were merely chamber of commerce boosters. In other words, they were sympathetic to the business community. Bagdikian wrote, "Most show no comparable basic interest in illuminating and reforming problems affecting the mass of readers—the poor, the lower middle class, the consumer."[50]

At the same time, the public needs to be reminded that a controlled press or an overseen press is not good for a democratic society, especially if it is controlled or overseen by the government. However, the press needs to remember that in order to regain respect from the various factions of society, it must learn the various problems of these factions, then provide appropriate information that helps solve some, if not all, of those problems.

In a democratic society, the press has more than one function. Besides informing the people, it should teach them how and why certain problems and conflicts occur. The modern press has this responsibility. The First Amendment was written for this very purpose. So in order to remain free, the press will have to acknowledge this obligation and then act accordingly. Otherwise, the public as well as the government may demand specific revisions in legislation pertaining to the press.

NOTES

1. Michael Emery, "Our Fragile First Amendment," *Readings in Mass Communication*, edited by Michael Emery and Ted Curtis Smythe (Dubuque, Iowa: Wm. C. Brown Co., 1977), 357.

2. Emery, "Our Fragile First Amendment," 357.

3. Emery, "Our Fragile First Amendment," 358.

4. Thomas I. Emerson, "The State of the First Amendment as We Enter '1984,'" *Freedom at Risk: Secrecy, Censorship, and Repression in the 1980s*, edited by Richard O. Curry (Philadelphia: Temple University Press, 1988), 31.

5. Emerson, "The State of the First Amendment as We Enter '1984,'" 31.

6. Emery, "Our Fragile First Amendment," 358.

7. Judith Schenck Koffler, "The New Seditious Libel," *Freedom at Risk: Secrecy, Censorship, and Repression in the 1980s*, edited by Richard O. Curry (Philadelphia: Temple University Press, 1988), 140.

8. Emery, "Our Fragile First Amendment," 358.

9. Emery, "Our Fragile First Amendment," 358.

10. Emery, "Our Fragile First Amendment," 358.

11. Emery, "Our Fragile First Amendment," 359.

12. Emery, "Our Fragile First Amendment," 358.

13. Emery, "Our Fragile First Amendment," 358.

14. Emery, "Our Fragile First Amendment," 358.

15. Jackie Harrison, *News* (New York: Routledge, 2006), 103.

16. Wilson Dizard, Jr., *Old Media New Media: Mass Communications in the Information Age* (New York: Longman Publishing Group, 1994), 64.

17. John L. Hulteng and Roy Paul Nelson, *The Fourth Estate* (New York: Harper and Row, 1971), 1.

18. Hulteng and Nelson, *The Fourth Estate*, 1.

19. William L. Rivers, Wilbur Schramm, and Clifford G. Christians, *Responsibility in Mass Communication* (New York: Harper and Row, 1980), 54.

20. Rivers, Schramm, and Christians, *Responsibility in Mass Communication*, 55.

21. Rivers, Schramm, and Christians, *Responsibility in Mass Communication*, 57.

22. Paul Gilbert, "The Oxygen of Publicity," *Ethical Issues in Journalism and the Media*, edited by Andrew Belsey and Ruth Chadwick (New York: Routledge, 1992), 158.

23. Rivers, Schramm, and Christians, *Responsibility in Mass Communication*, 62–63.

24. Hulteng and Nelson, *The Fourth Estate*, 301.

25. Donna A. Demac, *Liberty Denied: The Current Rise of Censorship in America* (New York: PEN American Center, 1988), 23-24.

26. Demac, *Liberty Denied*, 23.

27. Eve Pell, *The Big Chill* (Boston: Beacon Press, 1984), 162.

28. Pell, *The Big Chill*, 164–65.

29. Demac, *Liberty Denied*, 28.

30. Alan U. Schwartz, "Using the Courts to Muzzle the Press," *The First Freedom Today: Critical Issues Relating to Censorship and to Intellectual Freedom*, edited by Robert B. Downs and Ralph E. McCoy (Chicago: American Library Association, 1984), 282.

31. Andrew Belsey, "Privacy, Publicity and Politics," *Ethical Issues in Journalism and the Media*, edited by Andrew Belsey and Ruth Chadwick (New York: Routledge, 1982), 83.

32. Arthur R. Miller, "Overzealous Reporters vs. the Right to Privacy," *The First Freedom Today: Critical Issues Relating to Censorship and to Intellectual Freedom*, edited by Robert B. Downs and Ralph E. McCoy (Chicago: American Library Association, 1984), 285.

33. Clifton Daniel, "Fair Trial and Freedom of the Press," *The First Freedom Today: Critical Issues Relating to Censorship and to Intellectual Freedom*, edited by Robert B. Downs and Ralph E. McCoy (Chicago: American Library Association, 1984), 311.

34. Louis Nizer, "Trial by Headline," *The First Freedom Today: Critical Issues Relating to Censorship and to Intellectual Freedom*, edited by Robert B. Downs and Ralph E. McCoy (Chicago: American Library Association, 1984), 308.

35. Nizer, "Trial by Headline," 308.

36. Rivers, Schramm, and Christians, *Responsibility in Mass Communication*, 70.

37. Rivers, Schramm, and Christians, *Responsibility in Mass Communication*, 71.

38. Rivers, Schramm, and Christians, *Responsibility in Mass Communication*, 71–72.

39. Rivers, Schramm, and Christians, *Responsibility in Mass Communication*, 73.

40. Hulteng and Nelson, *The Fourth Estate*, 315.

41. Hulteng and Nelson, *The Fourth Estate*, 315.

42. Rivers, Schramm, and Christians, *Responsibility in Mass Communication*, 82-83.

43. Rivers, Schramm, and Christians, *Responsibility in Mass Communication*, 83.

44. Demac, *Liberty Denied*, 100.

45. Thomas I. Emerson, "The Danger of State Secrecy," *The First Freedom Today: Critical Issues Relating to Censorship and to Intellectual Freedom*, edited by Robert B. Downs and Ralph E. McCoy (Chicago: American Library Association, 1984), 258.

46. Richard Davis, *The Press and American Politics: The New Mediator* (White Plains, N.Y.: Longman Publishing Group, 1992), 121–22.

47. Dennis W. Mazzocco, *Networks of Power: Corporate TV's Threat to Democracy* (Boston: South End Press, 1994), 161.

48. Mazzocco, *Networks of Power*, 161.

49. Ben Bagdikian, "First Amendment Revisionism," *Columbia Journalism Review* (May/June 1974), 39.

50. Bagdikian, "First Amendment Revisionism," 46.

The Commission on Freedom of the Press and the New Canons of Journalism

This chapter discusses through the application of the charges and recommendations of the Commission on Freedom of the Press the degree to which the press is or is not fulfilling the goals set forth in the Canons of Journalism, which were originally written and adopted by the American Society of Newspaper Editors (ASNE) in 1922, then revised and renamed Statement of Principles in 1975 by ASNE. The chapter also discusses the changes between the original and revised versions.

THE STATEMENT OF PRINCIPLES (1975)

In response to the Commission on Freedom of the Press and its concerns about the press and whether the press is fulfilling the goals as set forth in the Canons of Journalism or Statement of Principles, the ASNE's Statement of Principles are presented first.

PREAMBLE

The First Amendment, protecting freedom of expression from abridgment by any law, guarantees to the people through their press a constitutional right, and thereby places on newspaper people a particular responsibility.

Thus journalism demands of its practitioners not only industry and knowledge but also the pursuit of a standard of integrity proportionate to the journalist's singular obligation.

To this end the American Society of Newspaper Editors sets forth this Statement of Principles as a standard encouraging the highest ethical and professional performance.

ARTICLE I—RESPONSIBILITY

The primary purpose of gathering and distributing news and opinion is to serve the general welfare by informing the people and enabling them to make judgments on the issues of the time. Newspapermen and women who abuse the power of their professional role for selfish motives or unworthy purposes are faithless to that public trust.

The American press was made free not just to inform or just to serve as a forum for debate but also to bring an independent scrutiny to bear on the forces of power in the society, including the conduct of official power at all levels of government.

ARTICLE II—FREEDOM OF THE PRESS

Freedom of the press belongs to the people. It must be defended against encroachment or assault from any quarter, public or private.

Journalists must be constantly alert to see that the public's business is conducted in public. They must be vigilant against all who would exploit the press for selfish purposes.

ARTICLE III—INDEPENDENCE

Journalists must avoid impropriety and the appearance of impropriety as well as any conflict of interest or the appearance of conflict. They should neither accept anything nor pursue any activity that might compromise or seem to compromise their integrity.

ARTICLE IV—TRUTH AND ACCURACY

Good faith with the reader is the foundation of good journalism. Every effort must be made to assure that the news content is accurate, free from bias and in context, and that all sides are presented fairly. Editorials, analytical articles and commentary should be held to the same standards of accuracy with respect to facts as news reports.

Significant errors of fact, as well as errors of omission, should be corrected promptly and prominently.

ARTICLE V—IMPARTIALITY

To be impartial does not require the press to be unquestioning or to refrain from editorial expression. Sound practice, however, demands a clear distinction for the reader between news reports and opinion. Articles that contain opinion or personal interpretation should be clearly identified.

ARTICLE VI—FAIR PLAY

Journalists should respect the rights of people involved in the news, observe the common standards of decency and stand accountable to the public for the fairness and accuracy of their news reports.

Persons publicly accused should be given the earliest opportunity to respond.

Pledges of confidentiality to news sources must be honored at all costs, and therefore should not be given lightly. Unless there is clear and pressing need to maintain confidences, sources of information should be identified.

These principles are intended to preserve, protect and strengthen the bond of trust and respect between American journalists and the American people, a bond that is essential to sustain the grant of freedom entrusted to both by the nation's founders.[1]

The preamble, which defines the First Amendment, declares that editorial employees of newspapers have a responsibility. (The Statement of Principles applies to broadcast media as well. In fact, recently ASNE changed its name to the American Society of News Editors.) That responsibility "demands of its practitioners not only industry and knowledge but also the pursuit of a standard of integrity proportionate to the journalist's singular obligation."[2] The obligation is to keep the First Amendment intact, without any stipulations passed by Congress. The six principles following the preamble define in abstract terms how editorial employees of newspapers and other media should perform when practicing their profession.

In the following analysis, each principle is critiqued in depth. Charges made in the report of the Commission on Freedom of the Press as well as other sources have been used extensively. However, before each principle is critiqued it is necessary to provide some information about the report.

Titled *A Free and Responsible Press*, the report of the Commission on Freedom of the Press appeared in 1947—twenty-two years after the original Canons of Journalism and twenty-eight years before the revised Statement of Principles. A committee of thirteen members heard testimony from fifty-eight men and women connected with the press; recorded interviews with more than 225 members of the industries, government, and private agencies concerned with the press; held seventeen two-day or three-day meetings; and studied 176 documents.[3]

CANONS OF JOURNALISM OR STATEMENT OF PRINCIPLES: A CRITIQUE

The committee found that the freedom of the press was in danger because:

> The development of the press . . . has greatly decreased the proportion of the people who can express their opinions and ideas through the press. . . . The few who are able to use the machinery of the press . . . have not provided a service adequate to the needs of society. . . . Those who direct the machinery of the press have engaged from time to time in practices which the society condemns and which, if continued, it will inevitably undertake to regulate or control.[4]

The committee believed that the above danger was due in part to: (1) the consequence of the economic structure of the press, (2) the consequence of the industrial organization of modern society, and (3) the result of the failure of the directors of the press to recognize the press needs of a modern nation and to estimate and accept the responsibilities that those needs impose upon them.[5]

Such criticisms attacked ASNE's Canons of Journalism or Statement of Principles, especially the first three articles. For example, the first paragraph of Article I—Responsibility conflicts with the committee's statement that those who actually can operate the press have not provided their services to the public. The committee realized that the press had not been responsible to the people.

Another example is Article II—Freedom of the Press. In the second paragraph, the second sentence reads, "They [journalists] must be vigilant against all who would exploit the press for selfish purposes." The committee believed that certain publishers had engaged in practices that the public condemns.[6] This, of course, concerns publishers who have selfish interests. Yet journalists seldom write about them in newspaper articles.

The committee realized, however, that government intervention was not the answer. After all, if the government intervened, freedom of the press could cease to exist—at least, as we know it. Nevertheless, the committee realized there was a drawback to the reality of free public expression. Indeed, even though one has freedom of speech and freedom of the press, there is no guarantee that a person who desires to speak will have an opportunity to do so; at least, not in print or on the air. Publishers and broadcasters determine who as well as what is read, seen, and heard by the public.[7] Of course, a person can communicate to others through e-mail or the social media. However, regarding communicating via e-mail, generally the person is communicating to an audience of one or a few, or, regarding communicating through social media, if there is more than one making up the audience, the person may not know the number receiving the message unless the person has hired a firm that has the means to determine the number.

The committee saw society needing, (1) "a truthful, comprehensive, and intelligent account of the day's events in a context which gives them meaning"; (2) "a forum for the exchange of comment and criticism"; (3) "a means of projecting the opinions and attitudes of the groups in the society to one another"; (4) "a method of presenting and clarifying the goals and values of the society"; and (5) "a way of reaching every member of the society by the currents of information, thought, and feeling which the press supplies."[8]

Regarding the first need, the committee stated that the media should not lie, that it should be accurate. In addition, the media should identify fact as fact. If opinion is provided, it should be identified as opinion. Furthermore, fact and opinion should be separated, not mixed.[9]

Regarding the second need, the committee asserted that newspaper industries should consider it their responsibility to (1) publish ideas contrary to their own, and (2) identify sources.

What the committee stated relates to Articles IV—Truth and Accuracy, V—Impartiality, and VI—Fair Play of the Canons of Journalism or Statement of Principles. However, note the differences. The committee's comments are more specific and concrete, not abstract like the Canons of Journalism or Statement of Principles (presented at the beginning of this chapter).

The committee believed that in small towns across the United States there were too many newspapers and radio stations owned by the same people, thus creating a *local* monopoly of local news.[10] It also believed that monopolistic practices as well as the cost of newspapers and broadcast stations had made it difficult, if not impossible, "for new ventures to enter the field of mass communications."[11]

Such practices may fracture Articles I, II, III, IV, V, and VI. As an example, in *The Media Monopoly*, Ben Bagdikian wrote,

> Most of the fourteen corporations that dominate the daily newspaper industry have acquired additional daily newspapers (and other media) in the last seven years. The number of daily papers in the country has continued to shrink, . . . but total national daily circulation has risen slightly . . . and is dominated by a smaller number of firms, from twenty-seven years ago to fourteen today.[12]

These fourteen companies owned more than four hundred newspapers. These newspapers accounted for more than half of the daily circulation of all newspapers published in the United States.[13]

Such statistics indicate that people are not getting enough sources of news to make judgments on the issues that confront them. Nor does freedom of the press belong to the people, but rather to a select few. Even if one gets most of his or her information from the World Wide Web, he or she is most likely viewing pages at a site that is tied to a traditional medium and its parent company, which probably owns other media (see the introduction). This author is convinced that independence of the journalist is limited due to the acquisitions of newspapers and/or other media by media conglomerates.

Truth and accuracy, impartiality, and fair play will, of course, be affected by such newspaper ownership. If what is being reported discredits a company that happens to be a part of the corporation that owns the newspaper, the story may not be published. As Ben Bagdikian wrote, "The important issue in the organization of journalism is not business monopoly or giantism in itself. . . . The central issue is how monopoly influences the flow of independent news and commentary."[14]

And what happens to truth, accuracy, impartiality, and fair play when newspaper companies are purchased by larger companies, say, cross-ownership companies? Bagdikian claimed that diversification and conglomeration created problems of economic power. He also claimed that the news could be affected when it was "controlled by corporations with deep non-journalistic financial involvement."[15]

In other words, these corporations may not care enough about journalism to consider the Statement of Principles. Impartiality could fail to exist. As Bagdikian put it, "Specific stories influenced by specific business interests cannot tell the whole story."[16] For example, newspapers belonging to certain families have been used to protect company and family interests. Bagdikian wrote, "Monopoly in communications decreases the chances that an interested party will notice and call attention to corporate conflicts in the news."[17] Without question, such is true. What corporation would allow one of its newspapers to publish an article contrary to corporate interests?

In *The Media Monopoly*, Bagdikian pointed out that General Electric, a major defense contractor, had purchased the Radio Corporation of America (RCA), which owned the National Broadcasting Company (NBC), for $6.3 billion.[18] The question that needed to be answered was whether the news department of NBC would broadcast a controversial story about General Electric's role as a major defense contractor, especially if the story depicted the corporation in a negative light. Bagdikian also pointed out that General Electric, like other large media firms, has, "through its board of directors, interlocks with still other major industrial and financial sectors of the American economy, in wood products, textiles, automotive supplies, department store chains, and banking."[19] Recently, General Electric and Comcast agreed that Comcast would control 51 percent and General Electric would control 49 percent of NBC Universal. Of course, this has to be approved by the federal government. It will be interesting if the news department broadcasts a controversial story about Comcast. For instance, Comcast's services for television, telephone, and the Internet, whether for homeowners or businesses, are not ranked as high as the same services offered by other communications companies.

Bagdikian claimed that interlocked boards of directors have potential conflicts of interest in the major corporations that control most of the country's media.[20]

In other words, because of these conflicts of interest, what is covered and how it is covered by those in the media will, in all likelihood, be affected. As Bagdikian pointed out, corporations now "own most of the news media that they wish to influence."[21]

In 1995, the Walt Disney Company purchased Capital Cities, which owned the American Broadcasting Company (ABC). At the time, the merger provided Disney with the following: Walt Disney Pictures, Touchstone Pictures, and ABC Productions; eleven company-owned TV stations, 228 TV affiliates, and twenty-one radio stations; ESPN and the Disney Channels on cable; newspapers in thirteen states; and Fairchild Publications and Chilton Publications.[22] In other words, the merger allowed Disney to have access to various media, not just film and cable.

Also in 1995, Westinghouse Electric Corporation purchased the Columbia Broadcasting System (CBS), another major television network with more than 200 affiliate stations.[23] Today, the CBS Corporation owns the CBS Television Network; CBS Television Stations; Showtime, a cable network; CBS Radio; CBS Outdoor, which offers outdoor displays to advertisers; and Simon and Schuster, a major publisher of books.

That same year the Turner Broadcasting System merged with Time Warner, Incorporated. This merger allowed one conglomerate to be in every aspect of entertainment and news—from producing films (Warner Bros. Picture Group), cartoons, and news to broadcasting the same on a multitude of cable networks such as Turner Network Television (TNT), Turner Classic Movies (TCM), Turner Broadcasting System (TBS), HBO, Cinemax, Cartoon Network, Cable News Network (CNN), Headline News (HLN), and others.[24] Time Warner also publishes various magazines, including *Time, People,* and *Fortune,* to mention three.

Viacom is another corporation that has holdings in television, especially cable television networks such as the various BET Networks and the various MTV Networks, not to mention film. The company owns Paramount Pictures Corporation.

News Corporation is another corporation that owns various media, including film, television, and print. Some of these companies include 20th Century Fox Film, 20th Century Fox Television, Fox Searchlight Pictures, Blue Sky Studios, Fox Broadcasting Company, HarperCollins Publishers, and various newspapers in Australia, the United Kingdom, and the United States.

The question that was raised earlier about NBC's coverage of General Electric could be applied to each of these marriages—that is, would the news departments of ABC and CNN broadcast stories that depicted Disney or Time

Warner in a negative light? Would CBS News broadcast a story that depicted the CBS Corporation in a negative light? Would one of Viacom's cable networks broadcast a story that depicted Viacom in a negative light? Would one of News Corporation's cable networks broadcast a story that presented the parent company in a negative light? The answer to these questions would be probably not.

In his book, *The New Media Monopoly*, Ben Bagdikian wrote,

> Today, none of the dominant media companies bother with dominance merely in a single medium. Their strategy has been to have major holdings in all the media, from newspapers to movie studios. This gives each of the five corporations and their leaders more communication power than was exercised by any despot or dictatorship in history.[25]

Bagdikian's five corporations consisted of Time Warner, The Walt Disney Company, News Corporation, Viacom, and Bertelsmann AG. The latter is headquartered in Germany and owns various media companies (Random House, Inc., RTL Group, Arvato, Gruner and Jahr, and Direct Group) that operate in numerous countries. Bertelsmann owns radio and television stations, newspapers, magazines, bookstores, online shops, and media clubs. The company publishes books in various countries. The company offers printing and digital, among other services.

These examples illustrate the potential problems when conglomerates get control of the media—that is, the Statement of Principles may cease to exist. Unfortunately, while writing about group and cross-media ownerships, the picture has not improved for newspapers. In 1983, for instance, thirty-six dailies changed hands; all but four became group units.[26] This trend continued into the 1990s and 2000s, as more dailies were purchased by large companies such as Gannett.

Article IV—Truth and Accuracy states in part, "Every effort must be made to assure that the news content is accurate, free from bias and in context, and that all sides are presented fairly."[27] However, the canon or principle does not define news. To the committee, news meant "something that has happened within the last few hours which will attract the interest of the customers."[28] The committee's criteria of interest included recency, combat, proximity, human interest, and novelty, which, according to the committee, limited accuracy and significance.[29] The committee also claimed that the press emphasized the exceptional and the sensational instead of the representative and the significant in order to attract the greatest audience.[30] According to the committee, in order to attract the largest audience, every news story had to be written to capture headlines. The result was merely a series of vignettes made to seem more significant than they actually were.[31]

The committee claimed that the press was in a dilemma because it tried to please its audience at the same time that it tried to present an accurate picture of the day's events.[32]

Unfortunately, the committee's assertions were correct. The press has and will continue to do this more out of habit than necessity.

In the column "Newswatch," Thomas Griffith wrote about the murders of African American children in Atlanta. He wrote,

> Every violent death of a black child in Atlanta . . . is piled on to the city's total . . . by a press prone to declare and then contribute to a "climate of fear." It may be a kind of retribution that the press now finds itself involved in its own mini-"crime wave"—the faking of stories.[33]

Then he mentioned the *Washington Post*'s Pulitzer Prize winner Janet Cooke and her made-up eight-year-old dope addict story and the *New York Daily News* flashy young columnist Michael Daly and his made-up English soldier story. Both reporters were fired for their lack of journalistic ethics, but the firing should not have stopped with them. After all, an editor or two should have had the information verified for accuracy. Such carelessness on the part of editors should be inexcusable and not tolerated.

RECOMMENDATIONS OF THE COMMISSION ON FREEDOM OF THE PRESS

The commission recognized the problems of the press, so in order to help eliminate some of them it proposed the following recommendations to be implemented by the government, if necessary. The commission believed that in order for the First Amendment to remain in effect the government may have to (1) state its own case, (2) supplement private sources of information, and (3) propose standards for private emulation.[34]

The committee recommended first that the constitutional guarantees of freedom of the press be applied to broadcast and film. Second, the committee recommended that the government encourage the growth of the

> communications industry, that it foster the introduction of new techniques, that it maintain competition . . . through the antitrust laws, but that those laws be sparingly used . . . and that, where concentration is necessary in communications, the government endeavor to see to it that the public gets the benefit of such concentration.[35]

Third, the committee recommended that legislation be written whereby one who has been libeled might obtain a retraction, a restatement of the facts, or an opportunity to reply.

Fourth, the committee recommended that legislation prohibiting expressions in favor of a change in institutions be repealed.

Fifth, the committee recommended that the government inform the public about its policies through the media or, if privately owned media were not available, the government should develop its own media.

The committee also recommended that the government supply information about the United States to other nations through the media or, if privately owned media were not available, the government should disseminate such information through its own media.[36]

These recommendations have been adopted by the government. For example, in relation to the second recommendation, there have been antitrust suits by the government. The third recommendation has been adopted in some court cases. And part of the fifth recommendation has seen light in the Public Broadcasting System (PBS) and Radio Free Europe. Unfortunately, action by the government has brought government intrusion, which could have been avoided if the press had followed the Canons of Journalism or the Statement of Principles and heeded the report. The media have criticized the government for withholding funds for PBS and have opposed certain programs on ideological grounds. Yet, the media are guilty of the same actions. This undoubtedly supports the commission's contention that those who are protectors of freedom of the press also threaten that freedom.

The commission's recommendations for the press were:

1. We recommend that the agencies of mass communication accept the responsibilities of common carriers of information and discussion.
2. We recommend that the agencies of mass communication assume the responsibility of financing new, experimental activities in their fields.
3. We recommend that the members of the press engage in vigorous mutual criticism.
4. We recommend that the press use every means that can be devised to increase the competence, independence, and effectiveness of its staff.
5. We recommend that the radio industry take control of its programs and that it treats advertising as it is treated by the best newspapers.[37]

These recommendations were written for a specific reason—that is, the Canons of Journalism or the Statement of Principles was not followed by most newspapers. The commission believed that the agencies of mass communication were not serving the public interest. Rather, they were "building and transforming the interest of the public."[38]

For example, in its first recommendation, the commission believed that Articles I, II, III, and especially IV of the Canons of Journalism or the Statement of Principles were not followed. The commission stated that publishers and broadcasters must be receptive to ideas that differed from theirs and that they must share those ideas with the public.[39] Article IV—Truth and Accuracy states, "Every effort must be made to assure that the news content is accurate, free from bias and in context, and that all sides are presented fairly."[40]

The second recommendation has been taken to heart to a certain extent by various mass communication companies. However, one may ask if these experimental activities are worthwhile. For instance, the *St. Petersburg Times* of Florida was the sponsor of the Poynter Institute (formerly the Modern Media Institute) for years. The institute offered classes for practicing journalists, faculty who taught courses in journalism and other areas of mass communications, and college students. Since its instructors were associated with the *St. Petersburg Times* and other news organizations at the time, one may question what was taught. Did the subject matter support the status quo? Did it question the practices of the press? The same questions can be asked of other institutes that have ties to certain media companies or organizations.

Although the commission's recommendation is a good one, an external organization should oversee the activity for obvious reasons.

The third recommendation, like the first one, saw the need for more self-criticism by the press. The commission said that ethical standards would not be achieved if mistakes and crimes committed by certain units of the press were not revealed by other units of the press.[41] The press has responded to a certain degree. Various publications, such as the *Columbia Journalism Review*, monitor the press. However, there is a need for more publications to do the same. Yet, the number of reviews that were founded primarily to monitor the press actually decreased during the 1980s and early 1990s.

The fourth recommendation seemed to be in response to personnel not reading any of the six articles. The commission assumed that there was a need for an educated news staff. Apparently, many publishers had not seen such a need.

The last recommendation pertained to the radio industry and its control by its advertisers. The commission hoped that the electronic communication industry would be more like the newspaper industry—that is, it would not allow advertisers to control the news. Unfortunately, the commission thought newspapers had not responded to advertisers' requests. The truth is some small as well as large newspapers have and do.

The commission's recommendations for the public were:

1. "Nonprofit institutions help supply the variety, quantity, and quality of press service required by the American people."
2. "Academic-professional centers of advanced study, research, and publication in the field of communications" be created and that existing journalism schools should take full advantage of the resources available to them through their universities in order to provide their students with the "broadest and most liberal training."
3. An independent agency be established to evaluate annually the performance of the press.[42]

The first recommendation has seen reality in a sense. But it has seen it in the electronic communications industry. For instance, there are nonprofit organizations providing some quality programs for the Public Broadcasting System. But the majority of the public does not watch these programs. Whether these programs actually fulfill what the commission had in mind may be debatable.

The second recommendation has taken a longer time, but it has seen light to a certain extent. There are accredited programs of study in which students not only learn the fundamentals of journalism, but also receive the rudiments of a solid liberal education. Indeed, the accrediting body for colleges, schools, and departments of journalism—the Accrediting Council on Education in Journalism and Mass Communications—requires a substantial number of courses in liberal arts and sciences (see chapter 8).

Several attempts have been made to implement the third recommendation. Unfortunately, the agencies or organizations that exist, except perhaps for Accuracy in Media, are associated with the different media industries and thus are not independent.

CANONS OF JOURNALISM AND STATEMENT OF PRINCIPLES: THE CHANGES
The original Canons of Journalism had seven articles—one more than the revised version. This, of course, is noticeable by mere observation. But there are other changes that need to be mentioned.

The preamble or beginning in the two documents is different. In the original, the primary function of newspapers is given: "to communicate to the human race what its members do, feel, and think." This is the point. In the revision, the importance of the First Amendment is presented. Both introduce the demands of the journalism profession.

The first article is different as well. In the original, emphasis is given to "The right of a newspaper to attract and hold readers is restricted by nothing but . . ."

In the revision, the focus is on the importance of gathering and distributing news and opinion: to serve the general welfare.

The second article in the original and the revision are similar, except that in the revision journalists "must be vigilant against all who would exploit the press for selfish purposes."

The third article in the original and the revision are basically the same, except that the original version is more specific—that is, the fundamental principle is followed by two numbered paragraphs specifying what the journalist should not do. In the revision, the third article is more general and much shorter.

The fourth article in the original and the revision is different. The headings and the content are different. The original version begins with practically the same sentence as the revision, then mentions truthfulness, accuracy, and a sentence regarding headlines: "Headlines should be fully warranted by the contents of the article which they surmount." The revision eliminates "sincerity" from its heading. In regard to news content, the revision includes "free from bias and in context, and that all sides are presented fairly." It also includes other forms of expression, such as editorials, analytical articles, and commentary—not just news. A second paragraph advises that errors "should be corrected promptly and prominently." This is included in the original version, but in Article VI—Fair Play.

The fifth article in the original and the revision are basically the same.

The sixth article in the original and the revision is different in that the revision includes Article VII of the original. Thus, there is no Article VII in the revision. Besides the other difference mentioned in the last sentence of Article IV, the revision contains a paragraph that is devoted to confidentiality of news sources. The original did not have this.

RECOMMENDATIONS

As illustrated in this chapter, the criticisms and suggestions of the Commission on Freedom of the Press are good ones. Little attention is apparently paid to the Canons of Journalism or the Statement of Principles, even though they were revised years ago.

It is this author's recommendation to follow the suggestions of the commission, especially the following:

Through Government—Recommendations 1, 2, 3, 4, and 5

By the Press—Recommendations 1, 3, 4, and 5

By the Public—Recommendations 1, 2, and 3

This author has reservations regarding the second recommendation for the press. This author believes that mass communication industries or organizations should finance new, experimental activities in their fields. However, these activities should be monitored, investigated, or supervised by some external organization so that what is done is good for the public—not just the industry, organization, or medium sponsoring the activity. Perhaps members of the public—those who are not affiliated with the media—could serve as monitors.

It would be this author's recommendation, too, for those who plan to work in mass communications to learn the Canons of Journalism or the Statement of Principles. Without question, these are not discussed enough, or the press would be doing a much better job.

NOTES

1. American Society of Newspaper Editors (ASNE) (1922), *Canons of Journalism* (now American Society of News Editors [ASNE] [1975], *Statement of Principles*).

2. ASNE, *Canons of Journalism.*

3. Commission on Freedom of the Press, *A Free and Responsible Press* (Chicago: University of Chicago Press, 1974), v–vi.

4. Commission on Freedom of the Press, *A Free and Responsible Press*, 1.

5. Commission on Freedom of the Press, *A Free and Responsible Press*, 2.

6. Commission on Freedom of the Press, *A Free and Responsible Press*, 1.

7. Commission on Freedom of the Press, *A Free and Responsible Press*, 15–16.

8. Commission on Freedom of the Press, *A Free and Responsible Press*, 20–21.

9. Commission on Freedom of the Press, *A Free and Responsible Press*, 21–22.

10. Commission on Freedom of the Press, *A Free and Responsible Press*, 43.

11. Commission on Freedom of the Press, *A Free and Responsible Press*, 49.

12. Ben H. Bagdikian, *The Media Monopoly* (Boston: Beacon Press, 1992), 22.

13. Ben H. Bagdikian, *The Media Monopoly*, 22.

14. Ben Bagdikian, *The Effete Conspiracy* (New York: Harper and Row, 1972), 60.

15. Ben Bagdikian, *The Effete Conspiracy*, 64.

16. Ben Bagdikian, *The Effete Conspiracy*, 64.

17. Ben Bagdikian, *The Effete Conspiracy*, 66.

18. Bagdikian, *The Media Monopoly*, 23.

19. Bagdikian, *The Media Monopoly*, 24.

20. Bagdikian, *The Media Monopoly*, 25.

21. Bagdikian, *The Media Monopoly*, 26.

22. Michael Oneal, Stephen Baker, and Ronald Grover, "Disney's Kingdom," *Business Week* (August 14, 1995), 31.

23. Oneal, Baker, and Grover, "Disney's Kingdom," 31.

24. David Greising, Michael Oneal, and Ronald Grover, "Time Warner Turner: Nice Script, But . . ." *Business Week* (September 11, 1995), 40–41.

25. Ben H. Bagdikian, *The New Media Monopoly*, 7th edition (Boston: Beacon Press, 2004), 3.

26. "Group Ownership Trend Continues—32 out of 36," *Editor and Publisher* (January 1, 1983), 34.

27. ASNE, *Canons of Journalism.*

28. Commission on Freedom of the Press, *A Free and Responsible Press*, 54–55.

29. Commission on Freedom of the Press, *A Free and Responsible Press*, 55.

30. Commission on Freedom of the Press, *A Free and Responsible Press*, 55.

31. Commission on Freedom of the Press, *A Free and Responsible Press*, 56.

32. Commission on Freedom of the Press, *A Free and Responsible Press*, 57.

33. Thomas Griffith, "Fact, Fiction and Fakery," *Time* (June 8, 1981), 53.

34. Commission on Freedom of the Press, *A Free and Responsible Press*, 81.

35. Commission on Freedom of the Press, *A Free and Responsible Press*, 82–89.

36. Commission on Freedom of the Press, *A Free and Responsible Press*, 82–89.

37. Tom Goldstein, ed., *Killing the Messenger: 100 Years of Media Criticism* (New York: Columbia University Press, 1989), 177–79.

38. Commission on Freedom of the Press, *A Free and Responsible Press*, 92.

39. Commission on Freedom of the Press, *A Free and Responsible Press*, 93.

40. ASNE, *Canons of Journalism.*

41. Commission on Freedom of the Press, *A Free and Responsible Press*, 94.

42. Commission on Freedom of the Press, *A Free and Responsible Press*, 97–100.

Factors That Impact News

This chapter discusses the factors that are relevant to the question, "What is news?" Basically, these factors impact news. The chapter examines the structure of the print and broadcast industries, as well as the roles of advertising and public relations.

NEWS: A DEFINITION

The concept of "news" has been defined by numerous journalists and scholars. For instance, Joshua Halberstam, in "A Prolegomenon for a Theory of News," wrote, "News is about events, not states-of-affairs. News aims at current rather than past or future events. News is the report of an event, not the experience of an event."[1]

W. Lance Bennett claimed, "News is usually defined as *information that is timely, relevant to the concerns of its audience, and presented in a form that is easy to grasp.*"[2]

In their text, *The Complete Reporter*, Julian Harriss, Kelly Leiter, and Stanley Johnson defined news as:

1. an account of man's changing relationships
2. an account of actual events which disrupt the status quo or which have the potential to cause such disruption
3. an event of community consequence[3]

Michael Schudson wrote, "News is what is publicly notable (within a framework of shared understanding that judges it to be both public and notable). It is also a machinery of notation."[4]

John Fiske, in "Popularity and the Politics of Information," identified at least two kinds of news. These include "official news" and "alternative news." Fiske claimed that "official news" appeared in the so-called quality press and network television. He wrote, "It presents its information as objective facts selected from an empiricist reality wherein lies a 'truth' that is accessible by good objective investigation. Its tone is serious, official, impersonal and is aimed at producing understanding and belief."[5]

Fiske claimed that "alternative news" differed from "official news" in two ways: (1) "in its selection of events to report," and (2) "in the way it makes the selection and, therefore, repression of events explicitly political."[6]

Any newsworthy event has to have "intrinsic characteristics known as news values."[7] These include: conflict, progress and/or disaster, consequence, eminence and/or prominence, novelty, timeliness and/or proximity, and sex. Walter J. Ward and his coauthors, in *The Nature of News in Three Dimensions*, found three news dimensions: normality, prominence, and significance.[8] Each dimension contained one or two news elements.

The characteristic *conflict* may be physical. Such usually leads to injury and damage and is therefore newsworthy. However, the clash of political, economic, or social theories, or debates over issues such as atomic energy, may cause conflict of a different nature and be newsworthy.

Progress and/or *disaster* result when new inventions, new remedies, or new devices appear. Unfortunately, such progress sometimes leads to disaster, such as toxic shock syndrome, which was caused primarily by a new device that contained a harmful component. Of course, progress does not have to be disastrous to be newsworthy. And there are disasters not linked to progress that are newsworthy because they change or alter the status quo.

Consequence is newsworthy, especially if an event causes or is capable of causing a great sequence of events affecting many persons. However, consequence may appear in stories of conflict, progress, disaster, or other news values. It tends to be a measurement of all the other news characteristics rather than an intrinsic characteristic of the news event itself.

Eminence and/or *prominence* are newsworthy because names do make news and may change or alter the status quo. Big names make bigger news. When Grace Kelly died, newspapers all over the world published news stories, not because she had been an actress, but because she had been a princess. When Princess Diana was killed in a car crash, newspapers and television programs all over the world contained news stories because she had been a princess and because the public had grown fond of her.

Novelty or *unusualness* is newsworthy. If a person grows a 330-pound tomato, or is taken aboard an unidentified flying object, or has an unusual hobby, it will make news. People are interested in the unusual. And such events disrupt the status quo.

Timeliness and/or *proximity* actually measure the news; that is, distinguish news from non-news. They are measurements to be applied to news after it is recognized, to determine whether it is worth gathering and whether and where it is salable. Timeliness is newness. Proximity is where the event occurred—its location in relation to the reader or viewer.

Sex sells to a certain extent. It sells more when it is coupled with eminence or prominence, such as when celebrities have affairs, marry, or divorce. It sells more when it is coupled with conflict.

As we have seen, in order for something to be newsworthy it has to have one or more news values. And these news values have to disrupt the status quo and/or appeal to readers' or viewers' interests. Usually, they do both.

THE BUSINESS SIDE OF THE MEDIA

Like any other business, newspapers, radio stations, and television stations exist to make money. Conglomerate-owned newspapers and broadcast stations as well as broadcast networks exist to make money, too. Unfortunately, as a result of this purpose, news often takes a backseat to profits.

In order to attract large audiences and make more money, shifts in newspaper content have risen. According to John H. McManus, "Although newspaper people may consider their product to be news-centered, most of its content also is not news. About 70% of the average newspaper is advertising and some of its editorial sections are explicitly designed to entertain."[9]

In his discussion of popular journalism in newspapers, Colin Sparks claimed that newspapers

> tend to give more space to sport than to politics, stress more that extraordinary category "human interest" than economic life, concentrate heavily upon individuals rather than institutions, upon the local and the immediate rather than the international and the long-term and so on.[10]

Television news programming has changed, too, but not in the public's interest. Network news people have become "stars" in the sense that they make enormous sums of money. Their salaries depend primarily on their programs' ratings, not, unfortunately, on the quality of their work. This is evident in *what* is presented as well as *how* it is presented—that is, news that has little consequence is presented in an entertaining fashion. John Langer, in "Truly Awful News on Television," pointed out, "Television news is based on crude forms of commercialism; it is controlled by callous market-oriented managers;

it indulges in gratuitous spectacle and traffics in trivialities and dubious emotionalism; it corrupts journalistic values and integrity; it is exploitative."[11]

Where does this leave the public? Is it true that if the media have a business mentality they will injure mass communication's obligations to society? The answer is yes, probably. When publishers, editors, and journalists believe that their responsibility is to the corporation that owns the medium for which they work and not to the public, problems arise. As William Allen White mentioned long ago, they invariably take on the country club point of view. They become business leaders in their towns. As a result, the information they present may be distorted and in some cases false. Or their opinions may appear in the guise of news in newspapers or in news programs on radio and television. Fortunately or unfortunately, depending on one's perspective, many websites that offer news also include journalists' or writers' opinions.

How can this business mentality and the biases it fosters be eliminated? First, executives must become aware of their positions, not only of their positions in the work force, but of their positions—indeed, their roles—in society. Second, journalists—print as well as broadcast—must have a sense of professionalism. Indeed, they must understand the importance of the press in a democratic society. If they adhere to the codes for journalists or the codes for broadcasters, this will be a step in the right direction. Unfortunately, the National Association of Broadcasters Radio Code and the National Association of Broadcasters Television Code were cancelled in 1982. The Federal Communications Commission, while not cancelled, has all but disappeared. No longer does it look out for the public's interest.

STRUCTURE OF THE PRINT AND BROADCAST INDUSTRIES

The Newsgathering Process

A staff at a newspaper gathers information for news stories differently from a staff at a major television network news organization; however, there are some similarities. For instance, most staffs of news organizations meet regularly to discuss and decide which stories will be covered, which reporters will cover them, and where the stories will be placed or positioned. Newspaper editorial staffs will have regular meetings with the circulation staffs to decide which stories are most likely to attract the most readers.

Generally, an editor at a newspaper will assign a specific story to a particular journalist, taking into consideration the journalist's specialty or ability and his or her contacts. Sometimes a journalist will have an idea for a story and pitch it to an editor. The process is similar at a radio or television station or network, except a producer typically will make an assignment. In addition to regular staff reporters, newspapers will use material by freelance journalists.

When a story is assigned to a journalist, the journalist will be given a certain amount of time for the story. Consequently, the journalist will need to gather as much information as possible and write the story by the deadline. Depending on the story assigned, the journalist may refer to one or more press releases for information, or the journalist may attend a city hall meeting, visit the police station, or attend a court trial. Of course, if the journalist is investigating a story about the state or federal government, then the reporter may contact one or more state or federal offices for information. Reporters also have other sources such as press conferences, coroner reports, wire services, phone calls from informants, e-mails from informants, government reports, research studies, and experts, among others.

When the reporter has written the story, the story will be read by at least one editor if it is for a newspaper or producer if it is for radio or television before it is published or broadcast. The editor or producer will likely ask the journalist questions to make certain the information is accurate. The editor or producer may change the phrasing. The editor will write the headline for the story.

Typically, a news story will contain a lead that acts as a hook, which causes the reader to desire more. The lead generally contains the most important and latest information. Newspaper stories may contain color (descriptions of people, places, or events), which helps readers visualize who or what the stories concern.[12]

The Gatekeeper Function

News goes through many people before it is published or aired. Each person is a gatekeeper. He or she decides which stories will be reported. For example, the news source is the first gatekeeper. He or she decides on what (and how much) to give to the media. The source is selective. The reporter getting the information is the next gatekeeper. He or she has to decide what to present in the story. In television, camera angles have to be taken into consideration. If the report goes to a wire service, the wire service editor serves as another gatekeeper. He or she has to decide what to pass along to regional and state bureaus. Once the story is sent, a similar decision is made by yet another gatekeeper at the other end. When the story reaches the newspaper or television station, the story is one of many. In fact, according to Ben Bagdikian,

RAND field studies show that typically the gatekeeper receives five stories for every one he puts into the paper. In general, the larger the circulation of the paper, the greater the percentage of stories thrown away, since the larger papers, though they have more space, have even more sources of news.[13]

Since the major gatekeeper in the news media is the editor or producer (radio and television), in addition to determining which stories reach the public, he or she has to decide what emphasis to give the stories. Also, he or she has to decide where to place the story (which page and where on the page), and the type size for the accompanying headline. These decisions may seem difficult to the layperson, but one has to remember that newspapers are not filled with news. Indeed, RAND studies found that news fills about 27 percent of the total paper.[14] In other words, one could call the traditional newspaper an "ad rag" and not necessarily be incorrect, since advertising fills 54 to 67 percent.[15] This range may be considerably higher today, since income from advertising accounts for most of a newspaper's income. Indeed, as Michael Schudson noted, around 80 percent of a newspaper's income is from advertising.[16]

Regarding the selection of news, Doris A. Graber claimed that "what becomes news depends, in part, on the *demographics, training, personality, and professional socialization* of news personnel."[17] Graber claimed that news selection also hinged on the "*intraorganizational norms and professional role conceptions* of newspeople and on *pressures of internal and external competition.*"[18] In other words, a newspaper's reporters and editors compete for space for their stories, and news organizations, whether newspapers or broadcast stations, compete for audiences and advertisers.

Readers and viewers, consequently, must ask themselves questions when they read newspapers or watch television news programs. As Marvin Olasky pointed out, "A story should be examined in the context of an entire newspaper or program. Where was it placed? How much space or time did it receive? Was it treated as hard news or feature? Could it have been either? How did it compare in interest to stories given more prominent space or time, or less?"[19] Other questions readers and viewers need to ask include: Who was behind the story? Who benefited from the story? Who was harmed by the story? As Doris A. Graber pointed out,

Inevitably, the stories that are publicized represent a small, unsystematic sample of the news of the day. In this sense every issue of a newspaper or every television newscast is a "biased sample" of current events. Published stories often generate follow-up coverage, heightening the bias effect. Attempts to be evenhanded may lead to similar coverage for events of dissimilar importance, thereby introducing bias.[20]

Gatekeeper versus Advertising

Because of advertising, the gatekeeper has a difficult job. At most newspapers the advertising department determines the number of pages to be printed. Only after this does news receive its allocation (called the "news hole"). Unfortunately, because the number of advertisements determines the size of the newspaper, the number of pages may not be known until the last minute. This procedure can create chaos for the gatekeeper. For example, she may have to add or delete a story or throw out a whole page. This calls for rethinking on her part. Another problem is that the editor never sees all the stories before she makes her decisions. Therefore, she does not know how the total news report will look. To help eliminate some of these problems, most, if not all, newspapers have installed computer systems.

Also, certain days actually create an obstacle for the news hole. For example, advertising takes up more space on certain days. On the days when the news hole is bigger, most of the hole is not filled with late-breaking news; it is filled with stories that have little relevance to the readers' lives. This latter point is true of other days, too. In other words, seldom does the gatekeeper have time to include late-breaking news.[21]

Gatekeepers and Policy

Although the official news policy is usually vague and almost never spelled out to any journalist because of the taboo in the trade against tampering with facts, it is exerted in effective ways. Ben Bagdikian noted, "Editorial executives control the assignment of stories. . . . They decide whether the finished story will be used or not, and if used, with what emphasis and length, and whether or not the reporter's name will appear on it."[22]

Thus, editors and journalists can promote their values by what they assign and write. However, only the gatekeeper is in a position to promote his or her as well as his or her employer's values by selecting those stories that promote those values.

PROBLEMS WITH TELEVISION NEWS

Although newspapers have small news holes, television news programs offer even less coverage. First of all, most filmed reports of national and international news seen on television are the product of the three broadcast networks (ABC, NBC, and CBS). Of course, the few cable news networks such as Fox

News and Cable News Network offer footage. Second, network and even station news programs are restricted by time. As Edward Jay Epstein pointed out, between twenty and thirty subjects are selected each day as possible stories.[23]

A third reason for less coverage is that network news organizations are limited in gathering news. They depend on camera crews based in only a few major cities for most of their national stories. Of course, they can rely on their affiliate stations to provide some coverage, but most, if not all, stories produced for a local station's news program then fed to the networks are about a major disaster or something similar. Thus, the viewer gets few stories from few cities of the country. One must realize that there are stories that are worth national attention; unfortunately, some of these stories are not covered because of their location.

Television is often described as being immediate; that is, news executives sometimes say that the network organization has little opportunity to intervene in news decisions. However, as Epstein mentioned, "Some film stories are delayed from one day to two weeks, because of certain organizational needs and policies."[24] This allows the producer control over the stories, since it affords him or her an opportunity to screen the film and, if necessary, edit it. This may, of course, alter the story and, consequently, reality.

Because television is a visual medium, there are certain stories that tend to dominate news programs. According to Epstein,

> The types of news stories best suited for television coverage are those specially planned, or induced, for the conveniences of the news media—press conferences, briefings, interviews, and the like—which the historian Daniel J. Boorstein has called "pseudo-events," and which by definition are scheduled well in advance and are certain to be, if only in a self-fulfilling sense, "newsworthy."[25]

As a result, other stories of significance are not used.

The assignment of news stories for television is similar to newspaper in that assignment editors located in New York, Washington, Chicago, or Los Angeles request reporters to cover specific events. (Editors on newspapers assign reporters to certain stories.) This can (and does) have an effect on stories. Since generalists report most of the news aired, stories that require specialists may be reported incorrectly, thus reducing the credibility of the reporter and the network. It may even reduce the credibility of the source. In short, responsibility of the press has been overlooked.

There is another factor one has to consider. News events seldom are covered as they occur. Camera crews are not present. And some events cannot be filmed or taped or covered live because of weather or lighting conditions, or because of restrictions. For this reason, the setup interview is often used. As Epstein pointed out, this type of interview serves several purposes:

> First, it enables a news crew to obtain film footage about an event that it did not attend or was not permitted to film. . . .
> Second, the interview assures that the subject will be filmed under favorable circumstances—an important technical consideration. . . .
> Third, interviews provide an easy means of presenting an abstract or difficult-to-film concept in human terms.[26]

But it should be emphasized that these interviews contain more than "talking heads." The film footage behind the person speaking contains action. One must wonder if what one is saying is "lost" because of the action on screen. Often stories on economic news have film of a production line or some other aspect of industry as background. Does the viewer lose the report because of the film, which is not truly connected to the story? Or the person may be heard and not seen at all. Action, as producers see it, is necessary to television news. They claim that viewers are interested in more than a person speaking. Whether they are right is another question.

The coverage of news for television is further restricted by several factors. First, there are only so many camera crews for news. Although the Cable News Network advertises that it covers the world, in actuality CNN, like the other networks, is limited. It cannot possibly cover the world. The networks are not designed today to give importance to news. Second, it costs more to transmit stories for television from some places than it does from other places, even though this may cease to be the case in the near future because of numerous changes in communications technology. Third, network news organizations have limited budgets. In short, news is not that important to the networks. A network makes considerably more money from a prime-time program than it does from an evening news program.[27]

PROBLEMS WITH NONTRADITIONAL MEDIA NEWS

As mentioned in the introduction, more people are getting information, including news, from online sources, although most of these online sources of news rely on traditional media for their information. Nonetheless, nontraditional media are having an impact on journalism. For instance, traditional media have websites today. Not only do these websites provide information that can be found in print or broadcast form, but they offer people more such as weblogs (blogs), which were started primarily to allow interaction between the medium hosting the site and its users. Early blogs were written by journalists who worked at the medium and focused on newsworthy items. Today, however, blogs are written by bloggers who are more opinionated and partisan than journalists. Indeed, reputable journalists strive for objectivity, not the opposite. Are blogs a form of journalism? To this author, it depends on the blog. Others who study journalism may claim that all blogs are a form of journalism. Of course, these people may be thinking of editorials because many blogs have one similarity with editorials: the writers' opinions are presented. In fact, in many blogs nothing resembling news stories can be found. In one study, as much as 40 percent of the subject matter in blogs was nothing more than "my life and experiences."[28]

On the other hand, presidential candidates, like Barack Obama, have used the Internet and specific websites successfully to not only inform people about their agenda and even opinions, but to distance themselves from others.

THE ROLE OF ADVERTISING

In their discussion of advertising, Clint C. Wilson II and Felix Gutierrez wrote, "Since the goal of advertising is to promote sales and consumption of the products advertised, advertising agencies serve no moral code other than to promote the products as ethically as possible to stimulate consumption."[29] Advertisers depend on media to deliver their sales messages and the media depend on advertisers. After all, advertising pays the bills.

According to John H. McManus,

> For both newspapers and television, having advertising rather than consumers as the primary source of income means that the way to increase profits is to produce a product that has a minimal threshold appeal to the maximum number of demographically desirable consumers in the signal or circulation area. . . . The economics of newspapers and television favor breadth of appeal over depth.[30]

In other words, advertisers seek public attention, not public education. Thus, the news has to focus on topics that are interesting to the majority of readers/viewers and has to be packaged in such a way that readers/viewers find the news attractive. As McManus wrote, "Market journalism rewards sources who "feed" the media saleable content and penalizes those without "spin masters" to promote them, as well as sources who would be honest and those who might try to explain complexity."[31]

In newspapers, advertising makes up about two-thirds of total income. However, advertisements should be separated from the features, the editorials, and the news. Advertising totally supports the broadcasting industry. The

advertiser may buy or support a specific program, or a segment of time during a program. However, newspapers and broadcasting stations should not
allow advertisers to influence what is reported. Unfortunately, in some cases,
newspapers are intimidated by advertisers. As John L. Hulteng and Roy Paul
Nelson claimed,

> A group of disgruntled advertisers in a small town could very possibly withdraw
> enough advertising revenue from the local weekly publisher to put him in seri-
> ous trouble. . . .
>   Because they are aware of this possibility, many small town publishers tend to
> walk warily with respect to local issues and local advertisers. . . . Many weeklies
> do not carry any editorial comment at all.[32]

Thus, advertising can influence the news, especially in low circulation
newspapers and small stations. But large newspapers can be intimidated, too.
Fortunately, few compromise. Most publishers and editors realize they have an
obligation as well as a responsibility to the public. If they give in to advertisers'
demands, that obligation and responsibility will cease to exist.
    Phyllis Kaniss wrote,

> Newspapers may be willing to alienate an individual advertiser to produce news
> coverage that impresses their audience enough to ultimately raise circulation. . . .
>   It may also be that in the current structure of competition among the local
> news media, there are many cases in which an advertiser needs the local news
> firm more than the firm needs the advertiser. . . . In addition, in large media
> markets where newspapers have a broad and diversified advertising base, threats
> by any one individual advertiser may have a limited impact.[33]

Of course, there have been some cases in which large newspapers have
weakened. These cases stand out as examples and illustrate what advertisers
can do to newspapers.
    The broadcasting networks, as mentioned, depend totally on advertising.
Therefore, influence by advertisers is possibly greater, particularly at the local
affiliate or independent station. For instance, Marion Just, Rosalind Levine,
and Kathleen Regan learned that 53 percent of 118 television news directors
had been pressured by advertisers to run positive stories or to kill negative
ones.[34] News programs, however, may not be hit by advertisers like entertainment programs and special documentary programs are. For example, some
documentaries that have aired contained evidence both for and against the

issue discussed. Thus, the documentaries lost their purposes. As John L. Hulteng and Roy Paul Nelson explained,

> The influence of the ratings on the advertisers who paid the bills led to a homogenization of much of the broadcasting content offered during prime time. . . . Proven, crowd-getting patterns . . . were favored, and the unusual or the innovative got little encouragement. Material likely to be offensive to a principal sponsor was rejected or toned down.[35]

The last sentence is especially noteworthy. If a sponsor does not like a program, it is either re-edited or put away. This can, of course, alter news stories, but seldom does at the network level because this practice is contrary to policies of certain news programs. However, as A. Lee and Norman Soloman pointed out, "TV networks and print media are under tremendous pressure to shape their product in a way that best accommodates the needs of their advertisers."[36]

Every publisher and broadcaster should investigate every advertisement to make sure it is true and not deceptive. Again, their responsibility to the public and not to the advertiser should be their first concern.

Although the advertising industry, together with outside organizations, in 1970 formed the National Advertising Review Board to investigate complaints and deceptive practices, the media are filled with advertisements disguised as articles, "plugs," so-called public service information, and "advertorials."[37] Furthermore, it is unrealistic to assume that the National Advertising Review Board or its affiliate organizations such as the National Advertising Division and the Children's Advertising Review Unit, or even the Federal Trade Commission, which investigates complaints against specific practices, can successfully screen every advertisement created. Indeed, each board reviews very few because there are very few complaints. Yet, the public has been deceived by such material for many years. Perhaps advertisers realize that publishers and broadcasters, because it is reflected in their newspapers and in their programs, share their philosophy and therefore do not have to change their methods of persuasion. Nonetheless, advertisers have codes to which they should adhere.

THE ROLE OF PUBLIC RELATIONS

According to Hulteng and Nelson, surveys have found that one-fourth of the stories in any newspaper came from a public relations firm.[38] Scott M. Cutlip "found that 40 percent of the news content in a typical U. S. newspaper originated with public relations press releases, story memos, or suggestions."[39]

On some newspapers it is reasonable to say that half to three-quarters of the news content originates in a public relations office. What happens to the news as a result? It is distorted, perhaps even false. Public relations personnel serve their clients first. In other words, their obligation is to make their clients appear positive in the public eye. Responsibility to the public is not that important to them, since they are not dealing directly with the public.

What happens to the news when columnists and reporters are on others' payrolls? As with advertising, the news favors those paying for it. Although this practice is not as prevalent as it once was, some cases do occur and as a result other reporters and columnists are disparaged by the public. Publishing companies, broadcasting stations, and networks have taken a dim view of those who participate in this practice, too, which has helped considerably. However, broadcasters, particularly managers of local stations, are accepting so-called video news releases, which are produced by corporate public relations firms. According to Lee and Soloman, "hundreds of local TV stations, beset by budget and staff cutbacks, air these free, ready-made news releases, which look increasingly realistic."[40] People who work in public relations should adhere to the code established by the Public Relations Society of America. Of course, certain practitioners may be asked by their employers to bend the rules from time to time. In such instances, what are these practitioners supposed to do? This is a difficult question. Yet, it must be answered.

FAVORS

Journalists and publishers have accepted freebies on a regular basis for quite some time. However, since the Society of Professional Journalists included the following in its 1973 Code of Ethics, reporters and publishers have taken a different point of view: "Gifts, favors, free travel, special treatment, or privileges can compromise the integrity of journalists and their employers. Nothing of value should be accepted."[41]

Freebies, of course, can change how a news story is written. The reporter will more than likely take into consideration the fact that he or she was allowed to see the event free of charge. This may not be a direct bribe to the journalist, but it may be viewed as one by the public. And if the journalist allows the freebie to influence what and how he or she writes, the bribe has worked. The journalist's responsibility to the public has ceased to exist.

Although journalists have a Code of Ethics they should follow, apparently members of the U.S. Congress do not, considering the number of members who take "trips" that have been paid for by organizations and companies.

Unfortunately, the media does not do a very good job in covering this kind of activity.

MANIPULATION

Images are produced by advertising personnel and public relations personnel to sell products, ideas, and/or candidates for political office to the masses.

Millions of dollars are spent in getting the messages to the public. Political candidates are manufactured and sold by firms like any other product. Usually, these public relations firms try to create an image for the candidate, an image that people will like. These firms may help select the issues, but this function is secondary. Creating positive images is the primary function.

RECOMMENDATIONS

What does the journalist have to know in order to present news of value to the public? First, he or she has to be aware of such practices. For example, one has to cut through the professionally prepared speeches, which are filled with abstract terms, and interpret accurately and responsibly what the true intentions of a political candidate are. In order for a democratic society to exist, this is of the utmost importance. The people have to learn everything possible about the person in order to make a decision on election day. The journalist must not be influenced by commercials or professionally prepared news releases. He or she must realize that copy about a candidate, for instance, is like copy for any piece of merchandise; that is, it has been written to persuade—not necessarily to inform—the public.

Manipulators have been successful in the past, perhaps too often for the country's welfare. For example, Presidents Kennedy, Johnson, and Nixon were successful in manipulating the press. President Franklin Roosevelt and his charismatic personality influenced what and how reporters wrote for the press.

Many American journalists never seem to discern fact from fiction until it is too late. Often, it seems they are more concerned about their byline instead of their story.

NOTES

1. Joshua Halberstam, "A Prolegomenon for a Theory of News," *Philosophical Issues in Journalism*, edited by Elliot D. Cohen (New York: Oxford University Press, 1992), 11.

2. W. Lance Bennett, *News: The Politics of Illusion* (New York: Longman, 1983), 125.

3. Julian Harriss, Kelly Leiter, and Stanley Johnson, *The Complete Reporter* (New York: Macmillan, 1977), 29.

4. Michael Schudson, *The Sociology of News* (New York: W. W. Norton, 2003), 6.

5. John Fiske, "Popularity and the Politics of Information," *Journalism and Popular Culture*, edited by Peter Dahlgren and Colin Sparks (Newbury Park, Calif.: SAGE Publications, 1992), 47.

6. Fiske, "Popularity and the Politics of Information," 47.

7. Harriss, Leiter, and Johnson, *The Complete Reporter*, 29.

8. Walter J. Ward and Associates, *The Nature of News in Three Dimensions* (Stillwater: Oklahoma State University, Bureau of Media Research, School of Journalism and Broadcasting, 1973), 22.

9. John H. McManus, *Market-Driven Journalism: Let the Citizen Beware* (Thousand Oaks, Calif.: SAGE Publications, 1994), 24.

10. Colin Sparks, "Popular Journalism: Theories and Practice," *Journalism and Popular Culture*, edited by Peter Dahlgren and Colin Sparks (Newbury Park, Calif.: SAGE Publications, 1992), 38-39.

11. John Langer, "Truly Awful News on Television," *Journalism and Popular Culture*, edited by Peter Dahlgren and Colin Sparks (Newbury Park, Calif.: SAGE Publications, 1992), 113.

12. Alexandra Kitty, *Don't Believe It! How Lies Become News* (New York: The Disinformation Company Ltd., 2005), 38–39.

13. Ben Bagdikian, "The Printed News System," *American Mass Media*, edited by Robert Atwan, Barry Orton, and William Vesterman (New York: Random House, 1978), 171.

14. Bagdikian, "The Printed News System," 172.

15. Bagdikian, "The Printed News System," 172.

16. Schudson, *The Sociology of News*, 117.

17. Doris A. Graber, *Mass Media and American Politics* (Washington, D.C.: Congressional Quarterly, 1993), 114.

18. Graber, *Mass Media and American Politics*, 114.

19. Marvin Olasky, *Prodigal Press: The Anti-Christian Bias of the American News Media* (Westchester, Ill.: Crossway Books, 1988), 125.

20. Graber, *Mass Media and American Politics*, 140.

21. Bagdikian, "The Printed News System," 176.

22. Bagdikian, "The Printed News System," 180–81.

23. Edward Jay Epstein, "The Selection of Reality," *American Mass Media*, edited by Robert Atwan, Barry Orton, and William Vesterman (New York: Random House, 1978), 388.

24. Epstein, "The Selection of Reality," 390.

25. Epstein, "The Selection of Reality," 391.

26. Epstein, "The Selection of Reality," 393.

27. Epstein, "The Selection of Reality," 395–96.

28. Charles Beckett, *SuperMedia: Saving Journalism So It Can Save the World* (Malden, Mass.: Blackwell Publishing, 2008), 15.

29. Clint C. Wilson II and Felix Gutierrez, *Minorities and Media: Diversity and the End of Mass Communication* (Beverly Hills, Calif.: SAGE Publications, 1985), 125–26.

30. McManus, *Market-Driven Journalism*, 61.

31. McManus, *Market-Driven Journalism*, 195.

32. John L. Hulteng and Roy Paul Nelson, *The Fourth Estate* (New York: Harper and Row, 1971), 31–32.

33. Phyllis Kaniss, *Making Local News* (Chicago: University of Chicago Press, 1991), 51.

34. Marion Just and Rosalind Levine, with Kathleen Regan, "News for Sale," "Project for Excellence in Journalism," *Columbia Journalism Review* (November/ December 2001), 2.

35. Hulteng and Nelson, *The Fourth Estate*, 233.

36. A. Lee and Norman Soloman, *Unreliable Sources: A Guide to Detecting Bias in News Media* (New York: Carol Publishing Group, 1990), 60.

37. William L. Rivers, Wilbur Schramm, and Clifford G. Christians, *Responsibility in Mass Communication* (New York: Harper and Row, 1980), 125–26.

38. Hulteng and Nelson, *The Fourth Estate*, 286.

39. Lee and Soloman, *Unreliable Sources*, 66.

40. Lee and Soloman, *Unreliable Sources*, 65.

41. Society of Professional Journalists, Sigma Delta Chi, Code of Ethics.

The Concepts of "News Balance" and "Objectivity"

This chapter discusses the compatibility and/or incompatibility of the concepts of "news balance" and "objectivity." The chapter then answers a common plea found in letters written to editors of daily newspapers and often implied in surveys regarding people's opinions of the media: "Just give us the straight news—no comments needed—we'll make up our minds."

WHAT IS "NEWS BALANCE"?

News balance is the intentional act by a reporter to present both or all sides of a story. In the broader sense, news balance is the intentional act by editors to present news, both good and bad, in equal amounts. Of course, as William Rivers, Wilbur Schramm, and Clifford Christians pointed out, in order to obtain news balance, standards such as truth and fairness must serve as guidelines.[1]

Mitchell Charnley, discussing news balance, wrote, "As the reader's or listener's representative, the reporter must constantly strive to give each fact its proper emphasis, to put it in proper relation to every other fact, and to establish its relative importance to the meaning of the story as a whole."[2]

WHAT IS "OBJECTIVITY"?

According to Charnley, "Objectivity means that the news comes to the consumer untainted by any personal bias or outside influence that would make it appear anything but what it is."[3]

Minelle Mahtani, in "Gendered News Practices: Examining Experiences of Women Journalists in Different National Contexts," wrote, "The celebration of objectivity as a standard for newswriting forces journalists to erase themselves from their stories, distance themselves from their subjects, and adopt a consistent pattern of cultural neutrality."[4]

According to Michael Ryan and James Tankard, Jr., objective reporting

views the journalist as an important witness who writes an objective account of what is personally seen, heard or otherwise learned about. This approach emphasizes the straight news story, which is written without first person references ("I," "we," "our," etc.), and without the reporter's opinions.[5]

Stephen J. A. Ward discussed objectivity. He wrote,

The doctrine of journalism objectivity, with its stress on facts, procedures, and impartiality, is a hybrid of the three senses of objectivity. According to traditional journalism objectivity, reports are ontologically objective if they are accurate and faithful descriptions of facts or events. Ontological objectivity in journalism involves telling it "the way it is." Reports are epistemically objective if they adhere to good reporting methods and standards. Reports are procedurally objective if they present information in a manner that is fair to sources and to rival viewpoints. The ideal objective report displays all three forms of objectivity.[6]

Ward claimed that "six related standards" helped "journalists decide whether a report" was objective or subjective: factuality, fairness, non-bias, independence, non-interpretation, and neutrality and detachment.[7]

Howard Tumber and Marina Prentoulis, in "Journalism and the Making of a Profession," mentioned that objectivity separated the press from party politics and that it is related to truthfulness, factuality, completeness, and accuracy.[8]

"OBJECTIVITY": ITS CRITICISM

Charnley pointed out two conflicts of objective reporting. One is that reporters are human and as humans they cannot be totally objective. The other is that facts alone cannot present the true picture or understanding of life. Charnley wrote, "When objectivity collides with complexity, a good reporter should help the consumer see the objective facts in perspective; he should provide relevant background information to clarify the complicated news events."[9]

In his book *On Reporting the News*, William Burrows took a stronger stand. He claimed that total objectivity was impossible because reporters' perceptions were colored by their emotions and prejudices. Burrows wrote:

Even a reporter who makes desperate efforts at impartiality faces two problems. First, he must not only decide which information to put in the story, but which to leave out. The part that is left out might make the story more objective but there may be no space for it. Second, he must decide which element of the story gets the most "play" (emphasis) and relegate the rest to lesser play. News judgment is the decisive factor, but even the soundest judgment does not mean that all important elements in a story will be represented in exact proportion to their real part in it.[10]

In his assessment of objectivity, Tom Koch claimed that news could not be objective. It could, according to Koch, "be shown to be consistent, following a general pattern of presentation accepted, usually without question, by journalists and readers alike. . . . Further, mainstream journalism in all its forms is highly predictable in the way it organizes information."[11] Koch claimed that reporters covered events in set ways.

In essence, objectivity is questionable today. Some journalists, like William Burrows, believe that there is no such thing as objectivity. Other journalists believe that since we live in such a complex society, objective reporting does not allow the journalist to properly cover the issues. For instance, Robert Miraldi wrote, "Objective reporting does not allow for a lengthy repetition of what was reported before; it is episodic and fragmented, and the necessary connections to previous episodes are often lost."[12] In other words, Miraldi claimed that certain stories were ongoing, that specific events did not start and stop to fit the confines of a news story. Wesley G. Pippert noted, "'Objectivity' is often held up as a journalistic ideal. But emphasis on 'objectivity' can obscure truth at times. Objectivity may become the mere presentation of two sides of an issue in a way that distorts the proportionate importance of each."[13]

Dale Minor presented another side to objectivity in his book *The Information War*:

If there is a single dominant shibboleth in contemporary journalism, it is "objectivity." In tandem with full disclosure, its canons occupy a place in the presumed hierarchy of journalistic ethics comparable to medicine's Hippocratic oath. Unfortunately, it is a principle observed most often in the breach or to avoid the perils of seeking the truth, and it is often prostituted as an excuse for superficiality or as a cover for the less than true.[14]

In other words, whether objective or interpretative reporting is used by the reporter depends on the newspaper's editorial stance toward the issue.

According to Minor, even if a reporter believes he needs to balance a story, he should do more. He should interpret the issues for his readers. After all, his responsibility as a journalist is to them, not necessarily to the publisher.

Michael Schudson mentioned that the notion of objectivity has produced several kinds of criticism:

1. "*The content of a news story rests on a set of substantive political assumptions,* assumptions whose validity is never questioned."
2. "The form constitutes content, that *the form of the news story incorporates its own bias.*"
3. The form of a news story is seen "not as a literary form, but as a social form tightly constrained by the routines of news gathering. Here the argument is that *the process of news gathering itself constructs an image of reality which reinforces official viewpoints.*"[15]

Theodore L. Glasser claimed that objective reporting has three biases: it is "against what the press typically defines as its role in a democracy" (i.e., watchdog); it is "against independent thinking; it emasculates the intellect by treating it as a disinterested spectator"; and it is "against the very idea of responsibility."[16] Journalists are compelled to report the news, not create the news.

As we have seen, objectivity (and balance in some cases) has received considerable criticism. Because of this criticism, reporting has changed to some extent. No longer is objective reporting enough. Interpretative reporting is needed.

There is a small group of journalists who have become outspoken advocates of subjectivity. Subjectivity is based on subjective observation. Subjective observation, according to Jim Willis, "is one in which the observer does the defining, based on characteristics of the object as well as characteristics of the observer."[17] Unfortunately, as Myra Macdonald argued, there can be positives and negatives in subjectivity:

Subjectivity can take very different forms . . . and some of these may aid knowledge information. Self-reflexivity on the part of reporters and presenters enables better understanding of the discursive constitution of their account and dispels the myth of objectivity whereas a more egotistical presentation of the investigating self encourages an absorption in personality that is more akin to celebrity adulation.[18]

In addition, as Richard Keeble pointed out, "journalists' engagement with the issues they are confronting and their participation in the events they are recording can end up appearing self-indulgent."[19]

Subjectivity can be used to influence readers. Bob Kohn pointed out that the *New York Times* is all about influence. He wrote,

> The publisher and editors of the *Times* have made no apologies for infusing their editorial views into their news pages. The integrity of the paper, jealously guarded for over half a century, has recently been blemished with distorted reporting, made worse by editorial attacks on the First Amendment rights of millions of American citizens.
>
> In an ugly manifestation of their arrogance, the *Times* seems convinced that their opinions are correct and their solutions should be adopted as public policy. That would seem to be the only explanation for the unscrupulous means they have chosen to exercise their influence.[20]

Kohn then presented an analysis of so-called straight news stories from the *Times* to prove his argument.

Before the compatibility and/or incompatibility of the concepts of news balance and objectivity is discussed, the concepts' development is historically traced in the following section. Hopefully, it will shed light on what has been presented thus far and what will be presented later.

THE HISTORICAL DEVELOPMENT OF "NEWS BALANCE" AND "OBJECTIVITY"

First, let's look at the libertarian theory of the press and the men who developed it. John Milton expressed his libertarian ideas in the seventeenth century. Thomas Jefferson expressed his a century later. John Stuart Mill expressed his a century after Jefferson.

Milton's *Areopagitica* saw men as intelligent beings, capable of recognizing truth in an open marketplace of ideas. Jefferson saw newspapers as safeguards to society. He knew that if newspapers were free to publish without government censorship, citizens would be able to make responsible decisions. Mill saw the need for expressed opinions. He knew that if people were allowed to express their ideas, truth would eventually result.

News balance and objectivity were not necessarily considered. After all, in the free and open marketplace of ideas expressed by Milton, Jefferson, and Mill, objectivity was not a requirement for truth. Truth would come as a result "of various versions of an issue or event."[21]

However, because independent newspapers were purchased by other newspaper companies and/or conglomerates, Milton's, Jefferson's, and Mill's expressions regarding an open marketplace of ideas faded. Something other than various voices had to be used to present the truth. Thus, news balance and objectivity were born. Nonetheless, as Robert Miraldi pointed out, "The rationale behind objectivity lies in the libertarian concept of a 'marketplace of ideas,' where rational individuals form their beliefs based on their access to ideas and information."[22]

The notion of objectivity found its way into newspapers during the first half of the twentieth century, as reporters and editors realized that opinion had no place in so-called news stories. A few who have written about the history of objectivity claim that the penny press was the basis for the concept, but that it was not practiced by any reporters until the end of the nineteenth century. For instance, Jim Willis wrote,

> In the early stages of mass-circulation dailies of the nineteenth century, "objectivity" first meant a rigorous reporting procedure that was a reaction to—and hopefully antidote to—the sensationalism and jingoism of the press in the nineteenth and early twentieth centuries.[23]

It is true that truthfulness and accuracy were written about and discussed by journalists in the 1800s; however, objectivity as we have come to know it was not practiced by a sizable majority of journalists until the twentieth century.

During this period, large newspapers in New York and Washington captured readers across the nation. With the help of radio and then television, a national press emerged. News syndicates grew in numbers. In addition to the Associated Press and the United Press International, which at one time supplied about 80 percent of the news to newspapers and broadcast stations, there were almost 300 syndicates in the United States and Canada.[24]

According to the article "The New Concerns About the Press," during the 1960s many college-educated news personnel and critics complained about the low educational level of newspapers, especially the coverage of news. They claimed that the traditional newspaper "had a narrow and distorted sense of reality."[25] According to them, the traditional newspaper

> imagined that uninspired persons, routinely turning out stories cast in stereotyped molds, were capable of giving an adequate picture of the world. It conceived life as a matter of day-to-day actions largely devoid of larger trends or ideas. It defined the world as an exclusive assemblage of institutions, and it depicted events from their point of view.[26]

As a result of these criticisms, a new journalism developed. Staffs were upgraded. Coverage was broadened to include social problems as well as public affairs. Magazine-type articles appeared in widely circulated newspapers.

Finally, ideas and causes were played up by reporters while events were played down. Journalism had finally caught up with society.

However, this new journalism has created some problems. One is advocacy. Reporters sometimes push their ideas in stories; the requirements of fairness are forgotten or tossed aside. Another is calling editorials news stories; balance is discarded altogether in these cases. A third problem is that the press has not become as factually accurate as it used to be; at least, there is no evidence of it. Thus the press's credibility among the public is not as great as it once was, as opinion polls often show.

Traditional media's websites are not necessarily an improvement over the older product, whether newspaper or television station or television network, at least, as far as news balance and objectivity are concerned. As mentioned in a previous chapter, traditional media have encouraged their journalists to do weblogs (blogs) so that readers can interact, and blogs have become part of traditional media's websites. Unfortunately, time devoted to blogs and other sections of the website means that possibly less time has been devoted to news stories, or at least not as much time as the stories deserved. If this is the case, news balance and/or objectivity may have been sacrificed by the reporter. Today, traditional media's websites seem to be designed by architects who understand marketing. Many are flashy, like a carnival, with the proverbial bells and whistles. Just as *USA Today* has been compared to McDonald's and Jell-O for content length and color, these websites tend to have the same characteristics, except some have audio and video for some of the material. Indeed, some of the advertising is more informative (and entertaining) than the so-called editorial material.

(IN)COMPATIBILITY OF "NEWS BALANCE" AND "OBJECTIVITY," DEPENDING ON HOW ONE LOOKS AT IT

News balance and objectivity can be compatible. But, as we have seen, sometimes the reporter mistakes one for the other.

The standard news story, or "straight news" story, which called for the chronicling of fact—objective, factual reporting, dispassionately setting forth a series or group of facts with all authorities and sources noted—had become the standard form by the beginning of World War I.[27] But, as mentioned, this changed after World War II, the Cold War, and the 1960s.

Tom Wicker pointed out, "On politics and government, objective journalism reported mostly the contents of official documents, or statements delivered by official spokesmen."[28] Occasionally, this led to embarrassment. For example, President Johnson was reported to be the peace candidate; official sources had confirmed this. But when he led the nation into war the reporters objectively wrote that he had no choice; and the same official sources were quoted.[29] President Reagan kept the majority of reporters in the dark when he sent troops to Grenada. Later, he used the excuse that if the media had been informed such information might have caused more soldiers to be killed. Although certain members of the press severely criticized him for this action, the majority of reporters seemed to accept unquestionably this explanation. President George W. Bush promoted the idea that Iraq had weapons of mass destruction to members of Congress and the American people. Unfortunately, the idea was accepted as fact by many reporters.

Interpretative reporting is fine. But reporters have to make sure they use facts—verifiable facts—and not opinion. If they investigate a story and it demands in-depth reporting, they must make sure they explain what happened rather than accuse someone of causing it. They may clarify and even analyze in the story, in which case the focus should be on *why*. But they have to remember that personal opinion should not be in the report.

AN ANSWER TO A COMMON PLEA IN LETTERS TO EDITORS

In responses to surveys and in letters to editors, respondents and readers have pleaded: "Just give us the straight news—no comments needed—we'll make up our minds."

These people have a point: the reporter's opinions are not needed. However, newspapers and other forms of media are read, seen, or heard by people of all ages, levels of intelligence, and so on, so they need more than mere facts, especially if the stories are complex. They need interpretations, explanations, and/or clarifications in some of the stories or they will not understand the issues involved nor learn how these issues affect them.

In the simpler stories, straight news may suffice; the reader may be able to form his or her conclusions or opinions. But for most of the stories appearing today, interpretation is needed. This does not mean that the reporter's opinions become part of the reporter's interpretation, however.

RECOMMENDATIONS

Reporters should make sure that what they write is full, balanced, and fair. In other words, they must make sure that all the facts have been presented, that both or all sides to the issue have been presented, and that the report is fair or objective as much as possible; that is, the reporter's bias has been eliminated as much as possible. Opinion should appear on the editorial pages.

Management of the media should make sure that true and balanced reports cover all noteworthy aspects of society and not just one. In short, the media should not play favorites. It should cover the poor as well as—perhaps more than—the rich. The poor have more problems. It should cover the Native American as well as the African American, the Catholic as well as the Jew. It should strive to inform the people—even educate them to a certain extent—so they can weigh the facts and decide what is right or wrong, or what is best or worst.

NOTES

1. William L. Rivers, Wilbur Schramm, and Clifford G. Christians, *Responsibility in Mass Communication* (New York: Harper and Row, 1980), 143.

2. Mitchell Charnley, *Reporting* (New York: Holt, Rinehart and Winston, 1963), 25.

3. Charnley, *Reporting*, 26.

4. Minelle Mahtani, "Gendered News Practices: Examining Experiences of Women Journalists in Different National Contexts," *Journalism: Critical Issues*, edited by Stuart Allan (Berkshire, England: Open University Press, McGraw-Hill Education, 2005), 4.

5. Michael Ryan and James Tankard, Jr., *Basic News Reporting* (Palo Alto, Calif.: Mayfield Publishing Co., 1977), 21.

6. Stephen J. A. Ward, *The Invention of Journalism Ethics: The Path to Objectivity and Beyond* (Montreal: McGill-Queen's University Press, 2004), 19.

7. Ward, *The Invention of Journalism Ethics*, 19.

8. Howard Tumber and Marina Prentoulis, "Journalism and the Making of a Profession," *Making Journalists: Diverse Models, Global Issues*, edited by Hugo De Burgh, Foreword by James Carran (London: Routledge, 2005), 64.

9. Charnley, *Reporting*, 27–28.

10. William Burrows, *On Reporting the News* (New York: New York University Press, 1977), 39.

11. Tom Koch, *The News as Myth: Fact and Context in Journalism* (Westport, Conn.: Greenwood Press, 1990), 20–21.

12. Robert Miraldi, *Muckraking and Objectivity: Journalism's Colliding Traditions* (Westport, Conn.: Greenwood Press, 1990), 141.

13. Wesley G. Pippert, *An Ethics of News: A Reporter's Search for Truth* (Washington, D.C.: Georgetown University Press, 1989), 5.

14. Dale Minor, *The Information War* (New York: Hawthorn Books, 1970), 194–95.

15. Michael Schudson, *Discovering the News* (New York: Basic Books, 1978), 184–86.

16. Theodore L. Glasser, "Objectivity and News Bias," *Philosophical Issues in Journalism*, edited by Elliot D. Cohen (New York: Oxford University Press, 1992), 176.

17. Jim Willis, *The Human Journalist: Reporters, Perspectives, and Emotions*, Afterword by Col. Ann Norwood, M.D., Mary Walsh, and Penny Owen (Westport, Conn.: Praeger Publishers, 2003), 45.

18. Myra Macdonald, *Exploring Media Discourse* (London: Hodder Education Group, 2003), 75.

19. Richard Keeble, "Journalism Ethics: Towards an Orwellian Critique?" *Journalism: Critical Issues*, edited by Stuart Allan (Berkshire, England: Open University Press, McGraw-Hill Education, 2005), 57-58.

20. Bob Kohn, *Journalistic Fraud: How the* New York Times *Distorts the News and Why It Can No Longer Be Trusted* (Nashville, Tenn.: WND Books, 2003), 20.

21. John L. Hulteng and Roy Paul Nelson, *The Fourth Estate* (New York: Harper and Row, 1971), 58.

22. Miraldi, *Muckraking and Objectivity*, 140–41.

23. Willis, *The Human Journalist*, 46.

24. Hulteng and Nelson, *The Fourth Estate*, 134.

25. "The New Concerns About the Press," *Readings in Mass Communications*, edited by Michael Emery and Ted Curtis Smythe (Dubuque, Iowa: Wm. C. Brown Co., 1977), 202–4.

26. "The New Concerns About the Press," 202–4.

27. Rivers, Schramm, and Christians, *Responsibility in Mass Communication*, 169.

28. Tom Wicker, *On Press* (New York: Berkley Publishing, 1979), 3.

29. Wicker, *On Press*, 6.

The Purposes of the Media

This chapter defines and discusses the three major functions of the media, discusses the strengths and/or weaknesses of each function, identifies the function that is best fulfilled by the media, and identifies the function that is least fulfilled by the media.

THE THREE MAJOR FUNCTIONS

The primary purpose of a newspaper is to inform the citizenry who reside in its area of distribution, while the primary purpose of radio and television is to entertain the citizenry.

William L. Rivers, Wilbur Schramm, and Clifford Christians claimed that through news bulletins or on-the-scene broadcasts or advertisements of opportunities, one of the chief functions of mass communication is to help people watch the horizon.[1] Another is to persuade.

Thus the media have at least three major functions: (1) to inform, (2) to entertain, and (3) to persuade.

Information Function

This function is probably the most important of the news media, especially of the newspaper. It helps people learn about their environment. This function is primarily the "news" function of the media, especially of the newspaper.

However, what is "news"? According to Thomas Berry,

> First, *news is any printable story which, in the opinion of the editor, will interest the readers of his paper* (or the audience of his broadcast). Second, *news is always completely true*, or it is at least a set of facts that have been presented to the

reporter as truth. Third, *news has a quality of recency about it*. Fourth, *news has an element of proximity about it*. Fifth, *news must have some element of the unusual about it.*[2]

This information will, of course, vary from one time to another. For instance, on a slow news day, some event may appear on the front page of a newspaper that, on a busy news day, would not run the story at all. This information will vary from one place to another, too. For example, some types of stories that appear frequently in rural newspapers would seldom make a page in a metropolitan newspaper. Furthermore, this information will vary in how it is handled by various newspapers. For instance, several competing newspaper editors may agree that a given set of facts provides news, but they may disagree on the kind of news, facts to be omitted, and angles to be stressed. Such may be the case between a tabloid, a local weekly, and a daily and each one's coverage of a murder. The tabloid probably would use large photographs showing the victim (and blood). The daily probably would stick to the facts and use a smaller photograph or no photograph. The local weekly probably would handle the story from a local angle, perhaps giving names of relatives, friends, and so forth, if the victim or perpetrator was a resident of the immediate area.

The treatment of information should be straightforward, factual, and impersonal—if possible. Of course, reporters have specific constraints regarding news stories. For instance, most, if not all, news stories that are written follow a specific formula. Other constraints include deadlines and even sources. Also, information seems to be getting more complicated because of jargon, technical terms, and government gobbledygook; thus, reporters sometimes have to interpret the news for the readers.

According to Curtis D. MacDougall,

> To interpret the news it is necessary to understand it, and understanding means more than just the ability to define the jargon used by persons in different works of life. It involves recognizing the particular event as one of a series with both a cause and effect. The historians of the future, with their perspective, may be better able to depict the trends and currents of the present, but if the gatherer of information is well informed, through reading of history, the study of economics, sociology, political science and other academic subjects, and is acquainted with the attempts of other observers to interpret the modern scene in books and magazine articles, s/he will at least be aware of the fact that an item of news is not an isolated incident but one inevitably linked to a chain of important events.[3]

But what about slanting and coloring a news story? When the facts of a story are arranged so as to lead the reader to a desired conclusion, a news story is said to be slanted. In doing this, the reporter is concerned with the arrangement of facts. When some facts are stressed and other facts are made inconspicuous or omitted altogether, a news story is said to be colored. In short, "news is slanted when the writer has attempted to influence the reader by arrangement of facts alone; news is colored when the writer attempts to influence the reader by arrangement of facts and by choice of words."[4]

The journalist should ask when the news should be slanted or colored. Or, more importantly, should the news be slanted or colored at all? The journalist must use professional ethics when answering these questions.

According to Harold Lasswell, three important social functions are carried through the various levels of communication:

Providing a watch on the environment and alerting the public to threats or problems developing in the world;

Coordinating and categorizing the various elements of the social structure, so that members of the public can comprehend the forces with which they must cope to survive and prosper;

Handing on from one generation to the next the knowledge and ideas that represent our cumulative cultural heritage.[5]

Although Lasswell did not contend that mass communication media were fully responsible for carrying out these several functions, other media analysts, such as Schramm and DeFleur, have suggested that the media share increasingly in all three functions.[6]

As John L. Hulteng put it,

All of the various communication media are equally important to us in making sense of what William James called the "blooming, buzzing confusion" that surrounds us. By their headlines, by the placement and length of stories in the evening newscast, the media help to order in importance both events and personalities. They help us to categorize. Since we can't attend to everything that is going on, the media provides us with clues to those things of particular significance to us individually, so that we can focus on matters that affect us most nearly.[7]

Concurrently, consumers of news use selective exposure. They reject what does not square with their individual views of the world. They use selective perception. They accept what they want to accept. They also use selective retention. They remember information that enhances their views and forget information that does not.

Maxwell McCombs, Edna Einsiedel, and David Weaver wrote, "Media messages are transformed by people's personal experiences, their motivations and interest in seeking additional information."[8] In other words, how one interprets a message depends on one's experiences and characteristics. This, of course, includes selectivity as well as a host of other terms found in the literature about mass communication, psychology, and sociology.

The strengths and the weaknesses of the information function are presented later.

Entertainment Function

This function is served by mass media in various forms, such as comics, human interest stories, features, celebrity interviews, puzzles, and reviews in newspapers and magazines; soap operas, docudramas, movies, talk shows, game shows, dramas, plays, musical programs, so-called reality shows, and even news programs on television; music, interviews, talk shows, and news programs on radio; movies and plays in theaters; novels, nonfiction, and how-to books; and, of course, musical recordings of all kinds—from country and western to classical and opera. There are other forms of entertainment, particularly for television, but the primary concern here is the entertainment found in newspapers and the major television networks.

According to Jackie Harrison, "Today, the growth of cheap popular newspapers is criticized for . . . speaking to the reader as someone who should be entertained rather than engaged."[9] This statement is true to a certain extent; however, contrary to popular belief, early newspapers in the United States were commercial enterprises and consequently contained material that entertained readers.

Nonetheless, as mentioned, Rivers, Schramm, and Christians stated that newspapers inform while radio and television entertain. Since newspapers have very little space after advertising, most of the holes are filled with informational pieces. These can be entertaining, but to publish entertainment pieces just because some people enjoy them is not a valid reason for publishers and editors to insert such on every page of their newspapers. Many newspaper readers desire more. But publishers and editors, in order to get those readers who read a specific entertaining columnist or a humorous comic strip, will include these items in their newspapers. After all, another subscriber means additional revenue from advertisers. Besides, newspaper publishers and editors realize that people do not like bad or negative news all the time. The reader actually is enticed to most sections of the paper as a result of publishers and editors knowing what types of material should be in each section. Thus, not only does the reader see or read the comics, features, and columns, she also notices the advertisements. And this is important. Revenue from advertisements supports the enterprise.

The entertainment function, in addition to attracting specific readers and breaking up the newspaper, has to "be presented so as to be interpretable within the experience of the audience; it must appeal to audience needs and interests; and it must, so far as possible, be designed to avoid the hazards of noise and interference."[10]

As Rivers, Schramm, and Christians pointed out, receivers of entertaining stories must be willing to go along with the story or appreciate the character that never existed.[11]

This may provide the clue to the late Erma Bombeck's successful transition from newspaper columnist to television celebrity; that is, her stories basically were the same funny segments of life that viewers of television, like readers of her columns, enjoyed.

The entertainment function is an important one. It helps readers of newspapers, and it allows viewers to forget their problems while they watch others who have bigger problems.

Persuasion Function

The persuasion function, like the information and entertainment functions, has to get the message from the source to the receiver. However, it has to do more. In essence, according to Rivers, Schramm, and Christians, it has to cause members of the audience to, in effect, change themselves.[12]

If people have preconceived notions toward something or about something, it is hard to change those notions or even get people's attention. Since the mass media are supported by advertising, advertising of a persuasive kind has to be printed or broadcast. In addition to advertising, which is an obvious form of persuasion, the mass media may persuade people to buy or like or dislike something, even ideas, by other forms.

Most commercials are presented in an entertaining manner. Even the advertisements on the Internet can be entertaining, although many users find these advertisements intrusive. In fact, most users of the Internet do not desire any advertisements whatsoever. However, people have grown to accept commercials on radio and television. This does not mean that audiences do not have their guard held high. They do, but people who work for the mass media realize that their audiences come with needs that have to be satisfied. All the people employed by the mass media have to do is make the pitch relevant to the audiences and, of course, attractive. In short, the package has to have appeal. This sounds simple, but it is not. As Rivers, Schramm, and Christians pointed out, usually, it means introducing information that causes the receiver to reexamine her environment and subsequently reexamine her needs, relationships, and beliefs.[13]

In other words, as ideas or products are introduced, the consumer should be questioning her environment, or her needs and her ways of meeting them, or her social relationships, or her beliefs and attitudes.

There are other tactics that may be used to persuade. One is the threat, such as smoking cigarettes causes cancer. Unless this statement is supported by evidence—substantial evidence—people may not accept it. (Even if it is supported by documented evidence there will be people who do not believe it.) Of course, studies have shown that as threat increases, so does avoidance. In short, the reader or viewer does not want to be frightened, so she avoids the message; she avoids dissonance.

Before persuasion can occur, however, defenses against change in attitudes and beliefs must be broken. Then "the process of reappraisal and reorganization of attitudes"[14] must be initiated.

STRENGTHS AND WEAKNESSES OF EACH FUNCTION

Information Function

First of all, this author takes issue with Rivers, Schramm, and Christians's contention about radio and television programs. They stated that these media were designed to entertain. Not necessarily. It is only because of entertainment being introduced on radio and television (and then eating most of the time each medium was on the air) that this became true. For instance, Ted Turner, with his Cable News Network, proved that people will watch news programs if the news is packaged correctly—that is, presented in an entertaining fashion. After all, "action" stories are more likely to hold attention than "talking heads." Other cable news networks have followed Turner's lead. And radio certainly uses "sounds" within a story to attract attention. This holds true for all-news radio stations and networks. This author believes a medium's design is linked to what is first introduced in or on that medium, not the medium itself.

William L. Rivers raised an important point regarding the information function. He wrote,

All of us live in a synthetic world, and the synthesis is made largely by the news media. Even if we pay no attention to news reports, we learn from those who do. So awesome is the informing power of the news media that when they are in error, few of us ever learn of it unless the media themselves tell us.[15]

The last sentence is troubling. How many newspaper publishers and editors acknowledge their products' errors? Or if they do, where are the corrections printed? Because this function is so important—not only to the readers, but to the paper's credibility—errors should be either corrected or acknowledged immediately. Article IV—Truth and Accuracy of the Canons of Journalism or Statement of Principles should be remembered by the publisher and editors. Of course, broadcasters should correct their mistakes as well.

However, reporters and editors have another problem, a problem that confronts them every day: which event should be covered or written about, and which of the numerous stories should be published. As mentioned by Rivers, journalists cannot reach everyone with single reports; they must provide a wide range of reports. Consequently, they have to ask themselves, "What kinds of information do the American people need to promote and protect their own legitimate interests and to function as effective citizens?"[16] In order for journalists to answer this question, they "must recognize the degree of diversity in ability to understand and absorb information—and, of course, the degree of interest among individuals."[17]

Unfortunately, when journalists and editors try to answer this question, they sometimes forget about accuracy. In his book, *Between Fact and Fiction: The Problems of Journalism*, Edward Jay Epstein wrote, "Journalists are rarely, if ever, in a position to establish the truth about an issue for themselves, and they are therefore almost entirely dependent on self-interested 'sources' for the version of reality that they report."[18]

The reasons for this are that newspapers have: (1) strict deadlines, which limit the time that can be spent investigating a story; (2) a restricted number of news holes, which limits the space that can be devoted to elucidating the details of an event; and (3) fixed budgets, which limit the resources that can be used on any single piece of reportage.[19] This, of course, includes news personnel. The number of reporting positions has been slashed at most, if not all, newspapers over the past few years. Consequently, fewer newsworthy events are being covered (and the newsworthy events that are covered are not necessarily covered in depth).

As Epstein pointed out, "it would be unreasonable to expect even the most resourceful journalist to produce anything more than a truncated version of reality."[20]

Journalists, therefore, are trapped, so to speak. For example, they cannot compel a witness to furnish them an account of an event. Witnesses need only tell reporters what they deem is in their own self-interest, and then they can lie or fashion their story to fit a particular purpose without risking any legal penalty. Nor can a journalist test an account by hostile cross-examination without jeopardizing the future cooperation of the witness.[21]

This happened in 1969 when reports concerning Black Panther violence were published. The Black Panthers claimed that an organized campaign of genocide had been waged against them. The reporters closest to the group could not dispute this claim because it would jeopardize their access to certain Panther spokesmen.[22]

Journalists also lack certain technical information, which forces them to rely on authoritative reports or so-called experts for their information. Journalists cannot always identify their sources. When this occurs, they cannot necessarily document their sources' claims. Thus, their stories may not be corroborated by other so-called experts. Consequently, egregious errors may occur or remain.[23]

In essence, "daily journalism is largely concerned with finding and retaining profitable sources of prepackaged stories."[24] This was true even in the case of Watergate. For example, the press did not assemble the evidence; investigative agencies of the government did. Then it was deliberately leaked to the press.[25] The dependency on leaks therefore causes most of the problems in reporting. Since a reporter does not have the time to verify every piece of information, conflicts and disputes may develop. Thus, the reporter's reputation and the newspaper's reputation become questionable.

Epstein claimed that journalists were caught in a dilemma. He wrote,

> They can either serve as faithful messengers for some subterranean interest, or they can recast the message into their own version of the story by adding, deleting, or altering material. The first alternative assures that the message will be accurately relayed to the intended audience, although the message itself might be false or misleading. The latter alternative, while lessening the source's control over the message, increases the risk of further distortion, since the journalist cannot be aware of the full context and circumstances surrounding the disclosure.[26]

According to Epstein, the tension in the dilemma could be alleviated to some degree "if journalists gave up the pretense of being establishers of truth, recognized themselves as agents for others who desired to disclose information, and clearly labeled the circumstances and interests behind the information they reported so that it could be intelligently evaluated."[27]

Of course, the mass media's information function does have positive attributes. One, it does provide information of some kind. Even if it comes from other agencies, it keeps people abreast of what is happening. Unfortunately, people have to realize that what they read, see, or hear is what a specific newspaper, radio station, television station, or television network wants them to read, see, or hear. And what that newspaper, radio station, television station, or television network has presented to the public has been provided by a source. The journalist did not come up with it on his or her own. This truth also applies to websites that provide news.

Entertainment Function

The mass media provide entertainment in various forms, including news stories, and this entertainment serves an important recreational function. As Ray Hiebert, Donald Ungurait, and Thomas Bohn claimed in their book, *Mass Media II*, "They [mass media fare] provide emotional escape, create fantasy, and allow for physical catharsis necessary to renewal of the human spirit."[28]

Furthermore, audiences of the media "use music, film, television, novels, and magazine literature to meet their need for art; and this art literally improves the quality of life in our intense, crowded, increasingly urbanized society. Art brings 'beauty' to mankind."[29]

In newspapers, entertainment helps support a page. For example, instead of having a solid page of straight news, which probably would dull the reader's senses, editors try to incorporate features, amusing sidebars, human interest stories, and fillers. Even news stories can be made entertaining by a different style of writing.

Whether in newspapers or on television, entertainment can inform to a certain extent. For instance, a specific columnist in a newspaper or a miniseries such as *Roots* or *John Adams* on television informs the reader or viewer. *Roots* provided information about the history and problems of African Americans while *John Adams* provided information about him and his family as well as about the early years of the United States.

Editorial cartoons not only entertain but "take positions on issues, analyze and interpret events."[30]

Entertainment can help persuade. As Hiebert, Ungurait, and Bohn pointed out, "One must attract and hold public attention in order to persuade, and entertainment is often more effective than information in winning over an audience."[31]

Of course, the point should be made that the function performed is often determined by the receiver. What is entertainment to one person may be information to another. However, it must be remembered that whatever is presented in the mass media, the reader, listener, or viewer did not make the selection; the employees of the media did.

Without question, newspapers use the smallest amount of material that could be classified pure entertainment. Nonetheless, it is an essential part. As it has been pointed out, the *Washington Post* "for years published the largest number of comic strips of any newspaper in the country."[32] The primary reason: to help build its circulation.

Television's content is dominated by mass culture. (Some would argue that the content on the Internet is dominated by mass culture, too.) Most, if not all, of the millions of households in the United States own at least one television. Therefore, since so many Americans want to be entertained, and since these people purchase advertisers' products, television's course has been charted.[33]

The entertainment function is not without criticism or weakness. For instance, there is the question of whether entertainment—some of it, at least— caters to the lowest common denominator in the mass audience. If so, it may have a degrading effect on our culture. Of course, whether a person believes this to be true depends on his perspective at the time.

Persuasion Function

Each person interprets differently what she or he sees, reads, or hears. Therefore, in order to reach some consensus about truth, a free exchange of these interpretations must exist. This is the principle upon which our press is based. Unfortunately, because of the press's structure—cross-media ownerships and conglomerates—this is difficult for Americans to do.

As Hiebert, Ungurait, and Bohn pointed out,

> The growth of mass media as powerful and complicated institutions has made it increasingly difficult for individuals outside the media to protect themselves from massive propaganda and to raise their voices to persuade others. Must those who do not have access to the mass media be denied the right to influence others? Must they content themselves with being victims of the persuasive force of those who do have such access? This question poses one of the basic dilemmas of modern democracy.[34]

The persuasion function is strong and can be seen in any periodical or newspaper or on television, and heard on radio. The mass media are used by politicians to persuade the public to either vote for them or accept their ideas.[35] Barack Obama used the media successfully as a presidential candidate to persuade the public to accept his ideas and subsequently vote for him. During the second year of his presidency, however, he received considerable criticism by the media and the public primarily because his ideas and actions had failed to stimulate the economy. Only jobs tied directly or indirectly to the federal, state, and local governments were created by the stimulus package that President Obama had encouraged Congress to pass.

Persuasion is presented in stories related to business, government, hospitals, schools, religious organizations, and even the mass media.[36] In short, stories, programs, and advertisements have elements of persuasion.

Since "some studies of some media have shown that more than 50 percent of the editorial matter originated in press releases or promotional material,"[37] it is little wonder that much of what is published is "puffery, self-promotion, or a cover up of damaging facts."[38]

In an article that appeared in an issue of the *Columbia Journalism Review*, Joanne Ambrosio revealed that in the *Wall Street Journal*'s October 4, 1980, issue, "eighty-four stories were based on press releases . . . 45 percent of the day's 188 news items."[39] In addition, "in thirty-two of these examples, the releases were reprinted almost verbatim or in paraphrases."[40] It should be noted that this occurred years before the News Corporation purchased the newspaper.

What kind of reporting is this? And if this was a common practice of the *Wall Street Journal* in 1980, what is the practice today? Is this a common practice at other major newspapers? Do these newspapers readily publish news releases put out by companies or their public relations firms? Or do these papers question and then investigate? How many broadcasters accept material from public relations firms and broadcast it during their news programs? As mentioned in a previous chapter, broadcasters have accepted such material.

Of course, this practice is questionable and certainly needs to be examined at great length by every managing editor. After all, their newspapers' credibility will be questioned, especially if the information presented is merely favorable publicity for a company. On the other hand, leaders of businesses or governments may manipulate the media—they have in the past—to shape public opinion. In either case, false or biased information—no matter who was responsible—may persuade the public to believe an untruth to be true.

Perhaps the persuasion function of the press has gotten out of hand. Indeed, the press needs to examine its responsibilities to the public. An objective story may be impossible, but journalists could strive for a fairer, more balanced story than they are writing.

ENTERTAINMENT—THE BEST FULFILLED FUNCTION

Undoubtedly, the mass media fulfills the entertainment function the best.

Not only do the media, particularly radio and television, include entertainment in abundant supply, it is diversified. There are comics, editorial cartoons, satiric columns, advice columns, features, human interest stories, and more in newspapers. Some of this information is offered by newspapers via their websites. There are dramas, soap operas, movies, game shows, so-called reality shows, and more on television. In fact, most of television's programming is entertainment. Some of this programming is offered by networks and stations via their websites. For the person who enjoys only movies or music, there are special cable networks to which he or she may subscribe. In fact, as cable and other forms of satellite communications technology develop, entertainment will fill people's lives even more than it does now. (Just look at how quickly cell phones have evolved. Today, cell phones are similar to computers in that they offer consumers more than just the technology required to make a phone call. Young people, especially, seem to be lost without their cell phones and their apps.) On radio, entertainment fills the air waves. From various music programs to celebrity interviews and talk shows, entertainment occupies most of a radio station's airtime. In order to compete with other AM and FM stations, other program formats will be developed.

INFORMATION—THE LEAST FULFILLED FUNCTION

The mass media fulfills the information function the least.

As shown, this function is not necessarily fulfilled by the media as much as it is by those who supply the media with information. In other words, the media seldom get a story; usually, it is given to the media by some person who hopes to gain something. For example, a politician may grant an interview regarding a bill. Although the media get the politician's points of view about the bill, she has received free media coverage, which may help her in the polls, especially if the audience is receptive to what she said.

Another point is the failure to check news releases for inaccuracies or to paraphrase them.

A third point is the failure of reporters to write in a straightforward, stick-to-the-facts style. Often, they are obligated to their editors and publishers and producers to slant a story a specific way. This can cause problems; the reader or viewer may question the story's accuracy or the reporter's interpretation of the facts.

Of course, there are other "wrongs," but many have been mentioned.

RECOMMENDATIONS

In order for the press to correct the failures mentioned above, and those mentioned earlier, it needs to reexamine its role in a democratic society. Then the publishers, editors, producers, and reporters need to ask themselves if they are fulfilling that role to the best of their ability. If they are not, then appropriate changes should be made.

NOTES

1. William L. Rivers, Wilbur Schramm, and Clifford G. Christians, *Responsibility in Mass Communication* (New York: Harper and Row, 1980), 16.

2. Thomas Berry, *Journalism in America* (New York: Hastings House, 1976), 27–28.

3. Curtis D. MacDougall, *Interpretative Reporting*, 8th ed. (New York: Macmillan, 1982), 16.

4. Berry, *Journalism in America*, 51.

5. John L. Hulteng, *The News Media—What Makes Them Tick?* (Englewood Cliffs, N.J.: Prentice-Hall, 1979), 82.

6. Hulteng, *The News Media—What Makes Them Tick?* 82.

7. Hulteng, *The News Media—What Makes Them Tick?* 83.

8. Maxwell McCombs, Edna Einsiedel, and David Weaver, *Contemporary Public Opinion: Issues and the News* (Hillsdale, N.J.: Lawrence Erlbaum Associates, 1991), 65.

9. Jackie Harrison, *News* (New York: Routledge, 2006), 55.

10. Rivers, Schramm, and Christians, *Responsibility in Mass Communication*, 23.

11. Rivers, Schramm, and Christians, *Responsibility in Mass Communication*, 23.

12. Rivers, Schramm, and Christians, *Responsibility in Mass Communication*, 24.

13. Rivers, Schramm, and Christians, *Responsibility in Mass Communication*, 25.

14. Rivers, Schramm, and Christians, *Responsibility in Mass Communication*, 25.

15. William L. Rivers, *The Mass Media: Reporting, Writing, Editing* (New York: Harper and Row, 1975), 12.

16. Rivers, *The Mass Media*, 23.

17. Rivers, *The Mass Media*, 23.

18. Edward Jay Epstein, *Between Fact and Fiction: The Problems of Journalism* (New York: Vintage Books, 1975), 3.

19. Epstein, *Between Fact and Fiction*, 5.

20. Epstein, *Between Fact and Fiction*, 5.

21. Epstein, *Between Fact and Fiction*, 6–7.

22. Epstein, *Between Fact and Fiction*, 7.

23. Epstein, *Between Fact and Fiction*, 8.

24. Epstein, *Between Fact and Fiction*, 9–10.

25. Epstein, *Between Fact and Fiction*, 10.

26. Epstein, *Between Fact and Fiction*, 16–17.

27. Epstein, *Between Fact and Fiction*, 16–17.

28. Ray Hiebert, Donald Ungurait, and Thomas Bohn, *Mass Media II* (New York: Longman, 1979), 445.

29. Hiebert, Ungurait, and Bohn, *Mass Media II*, 445–46.

30. Hiebert, Ungurait, and Bohn, *Mass Media II*, 447.

31. Hiebert, Ungurait, and Bohn, *Mass Media II*, 447–48.

32. Hiebert, Ungurait, and Bohn, *Mass Media II*, 452.
33. Hiebert, Ungurait, and Bohn, *Mass Media II*, 450.
34. Hiebert, Ungurait, and Bohn, *Mass Media II*, 403.
35. Hiebert, Ungurait, and Bohn, *Mass Media II*, 408.
36. Hiebert, Ungurait, and Bohn, *Mass Media II*, 409.
37. Hiebert, Ungurait, and Bohn, *Mass Media II*, 414.
38. Hiebert, Ungurait, and Bohn, *Mass Media II*, 414.
39. Joanne Ambrosio, "It's in the *Journal*, but This Is Reporting?" *Columbia Journalism Review* (March/April 1980), 35.
40. Ambrosio, "It's in the *Journal*, but This Is Reporting?" 35.

Media and Minorities

This chapter discusses the areas in which television and the press have best served and least served the minorities of the United States.

AN EXAMINATION OF WHAT "MINORITY" MEANS

In *The Media Environment*, Robert Stanley and Charles Steinberg claimed, "The term 'minority' is one of those connotative expressions that is both meaningful and confusing at the same time."[1] Then they explained what they meant:

> We speak of a multiplicity of minorities in the American scene: cultural minorities, culturally deprived minorities, religious minorities. Minority frequently means roughly what those who use it intend it to mean. Furthermore, minorities are not cemented in hard and fixed stratified areas. There is considerable crossing of lines. An individual may be considered a minority group-member in one classification and not in another.[2]

The authors then provided a succinct definition of the term: "Generally, . . . minorities are those groups which do not enjoy the same privileges, do not have the same opportunities and are not accorded the same degree of power or, in the vernacular, 'clout' as so-called majority groups."[3] They provided an example of what they meant: "In the broadcasting media, . . . cultural minorities are those whose tastes are not given the same consideration by the program-makers as those majority audiences who are significant factors in the ratings and, therefore, in the economic success of the program."[4]

The above may explain why those network executives, although they may have realized the potential market of non-whites for advertised products, failed to appeal to this particular audience; they were insignificant as far as ratings were concerned.

DEPICTION OF AFRICAN AMERICANS AND OTHER MINORITIES BY TELEVISION

In her article, "Women and Ethnic Groups in the Media," Linda Mehr indicated that television executives became concerned with ethnicity during the 1970s. African Americans and other minorities began to appear in a wide variety of programs. For example, *Good Times, The Jeffersons, Sanford and Son,* and *That's My Mama* attempted to examine—mostly in a humorous fashion—various aspects of African American life. Other programs featuring African Americans followed. Other minorities, such as Puerto Ricans, Chicanos, Italians, Jews, Irish Catholics, and Asians, have appeared over the years in the following programs: *On the Rocks; Popi; Calucci's Dept.; Chico and the Man; Petrocelli; Rhoda; Beacon Hill; Kate McShane; Hawaii 5-0; Welcome Back, Kotter;* and *Barney Miller.* However, as Mehr pointed out, "Despite the obvious attempt to define these characters as 'ethnic,' there is in fact little that distinguishes them as such outside of color or name."[5] In fact, because the images were not really "ethnic," this may be the reason for the programs' popularity. As Mehr mentioned, the characters were not "interchangeable ciphers" either. They were "distinguished . . . by their roles and their individual personalities and quirks." Mehr claimed that ethnic minorities were seldom "depicted as top professionals." Neither were "they found only at the bottom or criminal end of the scale."[6]

Although these programs do not necessarily explore in any depth the unique ethnic qualities of minorities in the United States, they do permit ethnic characters to appear in a wide variety of roles and images. In short, minorities may be considered "token" in appearance, which is, of course, a quantity, not a quality.

In the article, "Minorities and the Mass Media: 1970s to 1990s," Bradley S. Greenberg and Jeffrey E. Brand mentioned that George Gerbner had found that African Americans "constituted 11% of the prime-time program characters, 9% on the daytime serials (a substantial increase in the latter), and were less than 3% on Saturday morning" during the 1991–1992 season.[7]

In the book, *Representing "Race": Racisms, Ethnicities and Media,* John Downing and Charles Husband wrote,

> In 2002, . . . African Americans for the very first time in history appeared on the screen in approximate ratio to their percentage of the population. However, . . .

this had no necessary bearing on the significance of their roles within the show or to the quality of the script. These might be walk-on and ensemble parts, not continuing characters, and in no case guaranteed the portrayals were credible or interesting.[8]

Although African American actors and actresses were hired for entertainment programs, they were not necessarily filling major roles. Yet, according to the report, "TV Audience Special Study: African-American Audience," which was released by Nielsen Media Research in 2005, in 2004 the typical African American household had more television sets than other television households. In addition, the typical African American household subscribed more often to a premium cable service for television viewing than other television households. Perhaps as a result of these sets and services, members of African American households watched more television than members of other households.[9] In 2004 African Americans watched programs such as *American Idol, Girlfriends, Half and Half, Eve, NFL Monday Night Football, My Wife and Kids, The Parkers,* and *All of Us,* to mention a few.[10]

African American actors and actresses tend to be prominently featured on only a few programs from the major networks today. (The BET cable networks have programs that feature African American actors and actresses, but these programs are seen by a very small minority of the population. For instance, in the fall of 2010, none of the BET networks had a program in the top ten among African American viewers.[11])

Greenberg and Brand pointed out that other minorities were seldom seen on television. They wrote,

> Hispanics remain rarely visible in any programming from the networks and are seldom found on reruns or on soaps. Although Blacks have achieved a noticeable presence, studies cited indicate that the overall numbers are confounded by concentration on few shows, very little cross-race interaction, and so forth.[12]

According to Tamara K. Baldwin and Henry M. Sessoms, Hispanics accounted for "only 2 percent of all of the prime time characters in television programs that aired during the 1994-95 season."[13]

For the most part, this passage applies to programming from the networks today. Only once in a while is a Hispanic actor or actress featured on a program from a major network. (The Spanish language networks have programs that feature Hispanic actors and actresses, but these programs are viewed by a very small minority of the population. For instance, in the fall of 2010, the top ten programs among Hispanics were broadcast on the Univision Network. However, fewer than six million people saw the number one program.[14])

Women, on the other hand, have a strong presence on television. Because television is a medium geared to and dependent on general audiences (and because women purchase most of the goods sold in the United States) television executives must be somewhat more responsive to them. Indeed, according to the *Nielsen Media Research 1992–1993 Report on Television,* "Women 55+ viewed the most among all demographics (12 hours 28 minutes)."[15] This was based on prime-time hours for an average week. Even today women watch more prime-time television than males.

This is certainly one reason for there being so many programs that cater to women. During the day, for instance, networks broadcast network- or syndicate-created or -packaged game shows, talk shows, and soap operas, although the latter have lost appeal and consequently viewers. Indeed, production of several soap operas has stopped because of low ratings. Most of these programs target women. Many of these programs have females in the lead roles or feature females who have equal billing with their male counterparts. During prime time, networks broadcast network- or syndicate-developed or -packaged situation comedies, dramas, and certain hour-long news programs that have a female in the lead, or at least have a female who has equal billing with her male counterpart. For instance, *Roseanne, Murphy Brown,* and *Murder, She Wrote* offered females in the major roles, and females had important roles in such programs as *Home Improvement, Everybody Loves Raymond,* and *Coach.* In the latter three programs, the males were depicted as stupid or idiotic, while the females were depicted as sane and intelligent. Today, females occupy lead roles or have equal billing in comedies, courtroom dramas, and police programs. Even in the numerous *CSI* programs females occupy important roles.

As Mehr mentioned, during the last few years television executives have taken steps in the right direction by offering various "images for both women and ethnic groups."[16]

Thus, television entertainment is the least of the three evils. In fact, as pointed out by Mehr, television programming has made strides toward the better when depicting ethnic minority groups, especially women. Nonetheless, there is room for improving programs that depict minorities. Problems caused by who they are could be dealt with within the program's time frame. This would help others understand the issues and perhaps help create climates in which solid relationships could exist. In the fall of 2010, the CBS Network introduced *Mike and Molly,* a situation comedy about two overweight white people. The question is: will viewers appreciate the humorous situations and the dialogue enough to keep the program on the air? Or will viewers find some of the dialogue insulting to people who have a weight problem? In short, will the program be criticized for its handling of a problem that confronts many people in the United States?

HOW MINORITIES ARE BEST SERVED BY THE MEDIA

Entertainment

The media have best served minorities by entertaining them. However, even this area raises questions. In other words, entertainment is perhaps the least biased area of the three purposes of the media—information, entertainment, and persuasion. For example, in the Nielsen report, "TV Usage Greater Among Non-Whites," non-white households' overall television usage "during October-November, 1974 averaged 52.1 hours per week, 16% more than in white households."[17]

According to the report,

> Non-white households . . . on the average have more persons, particularly non-adults than white households. . . . Non-whites outviewed whites on both a household basis and among persons during all times except the mid-evening hours. During prime time, on a household basis, the average network program rating for non-whites was only 5% lower than among white households. Persons ratings, however, were 16-22% lower among non-whites during prime time. During weekday daytime the average network program rated 24-37% higher among non-whites both on a household and adult person basis.[18]

Network executives should have realized the potential market for advertised products—that is, a market that was willing to purchase products advertised during these closely watched programs. Of course, the advertisements or commercials would have had greater significance if African American actors and actresses had specific roles. However, during this period of 1974, one seldom saw commercials targeting the African American audience. In fact, few programs had an actor or actress that was African American.

In 1993, according to the *Nielsen Media Research 1992–1993 Report on Television*, "Among the three dayparts" (daytime, prime time, late night) "and four audience demographics" (women 18+, men 18+, teens 12–17, kids 2–11) "reported, African Americans viewed more than the All Other group in every daypart."[19]

According to the report,

> In primetime, African American households had their TV sets on two hours more than All Other households, and children 2-11 in African American households viewed 55% more than children 2-11 in All Other households.
>
> Daytime showed African American households viewing 59% more than All Other households, with men 18+ in African American households viewing 90% more than men 18+ in the All Other group. The largest difference in viewing among African American and All Other households was in late night—African American households viewed 87% more in that daypart.[20]

According to the report, "Among African American households and persons in African American households, situation comedies outranked all other programming."[21] The top-ranked network programs among African American households in 1992–1993 included *Fresh Prince of Bel Air, Roc, Martin, In Living Color, Blossom, A Different World, ILC First Season, Out All Night, Where I Live,* and *Hangin' with Mr. Cooper.*[22] Studies have indicated that African Americans have been attracted to programs with African American actors and actresses. This fact was evident in the top-ranked network programs mentioned above. Indeed, most of these programs featured African American actors and actresses and concerned humorous situations. However, most of the commercials shown during these programs were not necessarily targeting African American viewers. Only a few of these commercials had African American actors and actresses, for instance.

Today, as it was several years ago, members of African American television households as well as members of Hispanic television households watch more television than members of other television households. Whether this trend continues may be dependent upon several variables, not just programs having actors and actresses who represent specific minorities. For instance, people have more electronic gadgets, as pointed out by the "Television, Internet and Mobile Usage in the US: Three Screen Report," which was released in 2010. When the report was published, more than 60 percent of the households in the United States had broadband Internet access and almost 25 percent had smart phones.[23] At the time more than 50 percent of the households had a high-definition television and more than 33 percent had a digital video recorder.[24] Both of these encouraged people to watch television. As the report indicated, people did. In fact, between 2009 and 2010, the typical viewer increased the amount of time by two hours a month she or he sat in front of television.[25] The typical viewer watched more than 158 hours of programs in his or her home each month.[26] This did not include the time she or he spent viewing programs via other means (computer, smart phone, etc.).

HOW MINORITIES ARE LEAST SERVED

Information

News is the area that least serves minorities, both on television and in newspapers. For instance, the study, "The News as if All People Mattered," found that the media attempt to explain conflicts in simplistic terms—that is, one side versus another. This "often results, advertently or inadvertently, in news coverage that polarizes."[27]

According to the study,

The media further stimulate polarization by such action as treating subgroups within communities of interest differently, repeating inflammatory comments without challenge or balancing statements, omission of relevant news, disregard for certain communities, quoting and referencing sources predominantly from one subgroup.[28]

In other words, minorities, including women, are not depicted the same as their male counterparts. The report suggested that the composition of media staffs needed to represent society. Thus, more minorities, including women, needed to be hired. In addition, the concept of "newsworthiness" needed to be reexamined.

The problem of polarization may even be greater than one realizes. Most people in this country get their news from television and the Internet, but television news has a tendency to exaggerate. For instance, Mark Fitzgerald, in "Covering Crime in Black and White," wrote about Unity '94, which was sponsored by the Freedom Forum Foundation and concerned minorities and the press. Certain panelists, such as Charles Ogletree, pointed out, "Ninety-nine percent of black people don't commit crimes and yet we see images of black people day in, day out, and the impression is that they are all committing crimes."[29]

Robert M. Entman conducted a study that basically supported Ogletree's contention. In "Blacks in the News: Television, Modern Racism and Cultural Change," Entman examined news coverage by four television stations in Chicago to determine whether crime and political reporting depicted blacks as more physically threatening and demanding than their white counterparts. Entman found "that exposure over time to local TV news presents viewers with an accumulation of images that make blacks appear consistently threatening, demanding and undeserving of accommodation by government."[30]

Robert M. Entman and Andrew Rojecki studied the stories presented on the evening news programs of the major television networks in the early and late 1990s. Their book, *The Black Image in the White Mind: Media and Race in America*, was published in 2000. Entman and Rojecki wrote,

Media operators have growing incentives to rely upon sensational news of violence and crime—and sensational entertainment employing exaggerated or stereotyped role play. Those incentives are fed by norms of objectively detached profit seeking that legitimize providing public forums to the marginal, the extreme, and the conflict-ridden while denying much exposure—whether in news or entertainment—to the serious, quiet lives of the majority.[31]

The authors found that only 6.3 percent of the stories focused on activities of non-whites. African Americans were featured in 2.9 percent of the stories, Latinos were featured in 1.3 percent of the stories, and Asians were featured in 2.1 percent of the stories. Some 18.2 percent of the stories were ethnically mixed—that is, at least one person of an ethnic minority was involved in the stories. However, most stories (75.5 percent) focused exclusively on whites.[32] African Americans were found in human-interest stories, sports and entertainment stories, and discrimination stories.[33]

According to Clint C. Wilson II, Felix Gutierrez, and Lena M. Chao, excluding minorities from the news media indicates their position in society. They wrote, "Lack of coverage of peoples of color in mainstream news media had the effect of asserting their lack of status, a powerful psychological message delivered to whites and non-whites alike."[34]

However, African Americans have not been the only minority that has been depicted in a negative light. M. L. Stein, in "Relentless Criticism," reported on two panels that criticized the media for the way specific minorities, particularly Koreans, were depicted, especially by the media in California.[35]

Of course, who is covered and how may not be out of the ordinary. As Robert Muccigrosso wrote,

> Television both shapes and, in turn, is shaped by the nation's temper, needs, and problems. Sometimes outdistancing, sometimes lagging behind the tempo of contemporary life, it usually has tried to respond to what seem to be the wishes of its audience. In part this has resulted from the exigencies of commercial broadcasting; in part it reflects an understandable and sincere desire to give the people more or less what they want.[36]

In other words, television will program whatever it needs to program to get a larger share of the audience. This accounts for the numerous changes in news selection and format as well as entertainment programming. This also accounts for the criticism that has been presented as well as the criticism that resulted when television decided to cover riots in the 1960s, 1970s, 1980s, and 1990s.

As Muccigrosso asked, "Did television coverage of the battles for civil rights in Little Rock, Selma, Oxford, and on the Freedom Marches serve to inspire blacks with renewed hope or only to augment a sense of racial division? Did it have relatively little consequence?"[37] Of course, these questions are difficult to answer. However, even though television reporters tried to cover these events, certain reporters, by what they presented, actually influenced others to become engaged.

For instance, in the early 1960s riots occurred in Harlem and Bedford-Stuyvesant, New York. These riots were covered by television crews, and, concurrently, helped foster these riots. Reporters conducted daily interviews with specific leaders who predicted another holocaust. Many of these leaders were without supporters. Nonetheless, their words ultimately convinced those who lived in these areas that violence was imminent.

In the mid-1960s, riots erupted in Watts, a Los Angeles neighborhood. Television news crews responded and broadcast footage that, according to specific critics, helped influence others to become active participants.

In the late 1960s, riots occurred in fifteen cities in the United States, including Newark, New Jersey, and Detroit, Michigan. Although Detroit's television stations reacted in a positive manner by blacking out certain coverage, the city's police commissioner claimed that television stations could have informed people to stay away from specific sections of the city.

As a result of these riots, the President's Commission on Civil Disorders was formed. Headed by Illinois Governor Otto Kerner, the commission drew three conclusions: (1) the medium had tried to give a balanced version of the riots, despite various inaccuracies and misrepresentations; (2) it had exaggerated events; and (3) it had "failed to report . . . on the causes and consequences of civil disorders and the underlying problems of race relations."[38]

The Commission on Civil Disorders recommended that newspapers should discuss in a positive manner African Americans and their activities in every section. The commission recommended that television networks and stations should develop positive programs about African Americans.[39]

Although the press examined itself after these riots, it was guilty of the same charges in the late 1970s and early 1980s when rioting occurred in South Florida. For example, Miami television stations provided viewers with coverage of the burning and destruction of property as well as shootouts between African Americans and police. Television networks devoted several minutes to these events each evening.

In the late 1980s and early 1990s, riots occurred in Los Angeles. News crews from local independent television stations as well as network affiliates broadcasted the violence, which included several people getting killed. Such reporting was severely criticized by Koreans who had owned and/or operated stores in the area as well as by certain African Americans who had been directly involved. Certain authorities also condemned the coverage and claimed that television had exacerbated the problem.

The question is, does this sort of coverage actually inform or educate viewers, or does it incite some to participate, to riot? Another question is, does this kind of coverage label specific ethnic groups—does it stereotype them?

The Commission on Civil Disorders recommended that members of minorities be hired by the media. In 1996 D. H. Weaver and G. Cleveland Wilhoit reported that racial minorities held only 12 percent of the estimated 43,000 journalist positions.[40] In 2008 the American Society of News Editors (ASNE) found that racial minorities filled only 13.5 percent of the more than 52,000 journalist positions.[41] Unfortunately, these percentages were extremely low in both studies, considering the number of racial minorities in the overall population of the country.

NEWS AND STEREOTYPING: THE FIRST COMPLAINT

The media, especially newspapers and television, have employed stereotypes as shorthand means of communicating through headlines, copy, and pictures. Certain minority groups were (and are still, to an extent) often portrayed by symbols and stereotypes.

According to William L. Rivers, Wilbur Schramm, and Clifford G. Christians, if a news report is to be accurate, then it must not contain any language that stereotypes.[42] However, words such as "savages," "black uprising," "Communists," "terrorists," "riot," "rioting," "pigs," and "illegals," to mention a few, appear in print and are used on radio and television. News reports using such terms to describe or classify people do not help relationships between whites and nonwhites. Use and misuse of language has and will continue to worsen relationships.

According to Bernard Rubin,

> Stereotyping of minorities is still all too prevalent. Three researchers in Native American media coverage recently concluded: "Stereotypical misrepresentation in United States media of Native American peoples and cultures has been comprehensive and systematic since the 1880s. The methods of such stereotyping are known and the intent of their employment has been the effective dehumanization of the peoples depicted."[43]

Whether the media can overcome such problems as stereotyping is not the issue. The question is whether the media *will* overcome such problems. After all, most of the time it is much easier for a reporter or broadcaster to use a word or a phrase that everyone has heard to refer to a specific minority. As Jeremy Gerard, in "Can the Press Do the Right Thing? Hurting Words, Fighting Words," wrote, "Many civil libertarians acknowledge that what is called social censorship—in which the expression of prejudicial attitudes toward a group becomes unacceptable in civil discourse—is a phenomenon that may take decades to manifest itself."[44]

Only when the majority of readers or viewers expect reporters to use different words or expressions will such problems cease to exist in the media. As Linda Wright Moore wrote in "Can the Press Do the Right Thing? How Your News Looks to Us,"

> To cover communities that are increasingly diverse, journalists are going to have to bring to the story a knowledge of and sensitivity to different kinds of people and cultures. It is no longer acceptable to work from a limited personal perspective and yet claim to be objective.[45]

In addition to words and expressions, journalists use images to portray minorities in stereotypical terms. For instance, journalists have applied "war" paint to photographs of Native Americans for certain stories. They have used "mug" shots of African Americans, especially those who have been arrested. Such practices should not exist in today's media.

THE AVOIDANCE OF COVERAGE: THE SECOND COMPLAINT

The media seldom cover events in areas where specific minorities predominantly live, unless, of course, the event threatens the status quo or the established order. Stories about specific minorities that are used have been carefully selected and usually concern individuals of color who have escaped their designated place—that is, they have succeeded and therefore pose no threat to society.[46] Consequently, minorities criticize the media for lack of coverage.

Perhaps this is because media executives of the mass circulation organizations cater to the affluent, white majority and, as a result, consciously avoid placing stories about minorities.[47] The reason for them doing this is simple: they are afraid that what they publish or broadcast will adversely affect advertising revenue.

Otis Chandler of the *Los Angeles Times* received criticism in the mid-1970s from minority groups. At the time, African Americans, Latinos, and Asian Americans accounted for about half of the Los Angeles residents; however, the *Times* catered to the white, middle-class, and upper-class reader. Chandler explained that the *Times* did not target low-income readers primarily because it did not make sense financially to do so, since those readers could not afford the products advertised.

When an analysis of the *Times* readers was published in 1979, the *Times* staff created special editions in order to follow its readers. However, it failed to publish one for the various ethnic groups. Strides have been made by the *Times*, as Mercedes Lynn de Uriarte noted in the article, "A Problematic Press: Latinos and the News." At the time the article was written, the *Times* and the

Dallas Morning News led other newspapers in coverage of Latinos, including Latino politics. According to de Uriarte, both newspapers had hired members of minorities, including Latinos, for various journalism positions.[48]

Unfortunately, many other metropolitan newspapers serving areas that have large pockets of minority groups have failed. Boston is an example. Although it has a large population of Hispanics (from one-tenth to one-twelfth of the city's population), the media, for the most part, have failed in their coverage of this minority.[49]

THE LACK OF MINORITY-OWNED MEDIA: THE THIRD COMPLAINT

Although African American newspapers exist, many were verbally attacked during the 1970s. As Stanley and Steinberg pointed out,

> The "black power" movement has been impatient with the black newspapers, blaming their editors and publishers particularly for taking too placid a stand on crucial issues. The result has been the publication of a group of newspapers which are devoted less to hard news than to militant discussion of the necessary goals yet to be achieved by black citizens.[50]

The black press has other problems, too. One is the growth of television and the Internet, which has had an effect on white-owned publications, as well. Another is the high cost of printing. A third is the lack of trained African American journalists. (Or if they are trained they are usually hired by white-owned publications.) A fourth is the lack of advertising, which is detrimental to any publication. Although these are major problems, about 175 newspapers were published by and for African Americans during the late 1970s and early 1980s. Unfortunately, the content of these papers did not discuss the problems facing African Americans. In fact, the content in some cases was no more than mere press releases.[51] Today, there are more newspapers being published by African Americans. The content in these newspapers has progressed; problems of African Americans, for instance, are identified and discussed.

According to Joe Flint, "In 1976, there were 30 minority-owned radio stations and one TV station in the United States. The number ballooned during the Carter administration to 140 radio stations and 10 TV's."[52] In the early 1990s there were more than 180 minority-owned radio stations and more than 10 television stations.[53] Today, minorities own about 8 percent of the radio stations and about 3 percent of the television stations.[54]

Because the operations of these media cost so much, few African Americans and other minorities are in the position to purchase a radio or television station. However, some African American groups have purchased stations.

During the 1970s, for instance, more than forty radio stations were purchased by African American groups.[55] Unfortunately, in "Can Black Radio Survive an Industry Shakeout?" Matthew S. Scott wrote, "Black ownership of FM radio stations saw perhaps its biggest falloff ever, from 71 in 1991 to 64 in 1992. Although the number of black AM station owners ticked up slightly last year (from 109 up to 111), black radio still suffers from static in the industry."[56]

Scott claimed that during the 1980s and early 1990s, "the growth of black radio ownership stalled. The number of stations increased by just 25%, from 140 to 182."[57]

This problem seems to occur whenever the economy sours, which is understandable, or when one medium becomes more popular than others among buyers.

The Spanish-language press is not as great in number as the African American–owned press. In fact, by the mid-1970s there were only four Spanish-language newspapers published in the United States.[58] Although the number has increased, the number is extremely low compared to the size of the Spanish-speaking population.

The number of radio stations broadcasting Spanish-language programs totaled 485 in 1974; fifty-five of these broadcasted Spanish-language programs on a full-time basis. Although the number of stations has increased, the number is low compared to the size of the Spanish-speaking population.

About forty television stations broadcast part of their programs in Spanish.[59] It must be pointed out, however, that these stations were not necessarily owned or even operated by Latinos. They were, for the most part, profit-making stations owned by whites. There were, of course, Latino alternative media that were owned by community organizations or media collectives. These media provided information and analysis that were usually not presented in the established media.[60] In addition to television stations, there are competing Spanish-language television networks, including Univision, which broadcasts some of the most popular programs watched by Latinos.

The outlook for media owned and/or operated by specific minorities may be positive, as society becomes more segmented and certain minorities have greater percentages of the overall population. However, advertising revenues may never be as great in these media as advertising revenues are in other media.

MINORITY EMPLOYMENT

The media, in order to cover racial issues and minority news properly, need to hire minority members who know and understand what the racial issues are and how to present these issues to the public. All the readers of newspapers or listeners of radio stations or viewers of television stations must be informed; this is imperative.

How many newspapers, radio stations, and television stations hire members of minorities? In 1978, "75 percent of the newspapers had no minority employees. A scarce 4 percent of reporters and editors on dailies (approximately 1,700 individuals) were of minority origins."[61] And funds for minority scholarships had decreased.

The percentage of minority members employed by the broadcasting industries was no greater. In fact, in 1978 only 14.1 percent were employed in broadcasting.[62]

Donald L. Guimary conducted a study in 1984 that focused on newspaper and television newsrooms in California, and "found minorities comprising only 12.7 percent of newspaper newsrooms and 18 percent of major-market television newsrooms in the state."[63] However, these percentages were higher than "the national averages . . . of 5.8 percent minority representation in newspaper newsrooms and 14 percent in television newsrooms."[64]

As mentioned, these figures have increased. Of course, considering the populations of minorities in the United States, this percentage is still too low. For radio and television, minorities have fared somewhat better, but the percentages are still too low.

RECOMMENDATIONS

Changes have to be made in order to see quality reporting of controversial racial issues. Only those involved can tell those who are not involved what is real and what is not. If the press remains the same, it will not achieve its purpose, which should be to inform and educate the public. Members of minorities need to be encouraged to attend college to study the media. Media companies should offer more scholarships to members of minorities. Minorities who graduate should be hired by media companies and promoted just like other employees. Minorities need to be encouraged to serve in leadership positions, not just reporting, editing, or co-anchoring a news program.

NOTES

1. Robert H. Stanley and Charles S. Steinberg, *The Media Environment* (New York: Hastings House, 1976), 243.
2. Stanley and Steinberg, *The Media Environment*, 243.
3. Stanley and Steinberg, *The Media Environment*, 243.
4. Stanley and Steinberg, *The Media Environment*, 243.

5. Linda Mehr, "Women and Ethnic Groups in the Media," *Social Responsibilities of the Mass Media*, edited by Allan Casebier and Janet Casebier (Washington, D.C.: University Press of America, 1978), 113.

6. Mehr, "Women and Ethnic Groups in the Media," 114–15.

7. Bradley S. Greenberg and Jeffrey E. Brand, "Minorities and the Mass Media: 1970s to 1990s," *Media Effects: Advances in Theory and Research*, edited by Jennings Bryant and Dolf Zillmann (Hillsdale, N.J.: Lawrence Erlbaum Associates, 1994), 276.

8. John Downing and Charles Husband, *Representing "Race": Racisms, Ethnicities and Media* (London: SAGE Publications, 2005), 164–65.

9. Jana Steadman, "TV Audience Special Study: African-American Audience," Nielsen Media Research, Summer 2005, 11–12, www.nielsenmedia.com/E-letters/African-AmericanTVA-final.pdf (29 Sept. 2010).

10. "Top Primetime Programs—African-American Homes," www.nielsenmedia.com/ethnicmeasure/african-american/programsAA.html (29 Sept. 2010).

11. "Television: Among African-Americans—United States," http://en-us.nielsen.com/content/nielsen/en_us/insights/rankings/television.print.html (29 Sept. 2010).

12. Greenberg and Brand, "Minorities and the Mass Media: 1970s to 1990s," 305.

13. Tamara K. Baldwin and Henry M. Sessoms, "Race and Ethnicity," *Media Bias: Finding It, Fixing It*, edited by Wm. David Sloan and Jean Burleson Mackay (Jefferson, N.C.: McFarland and Company Publishers, Inc., 2002), 106.

14. "Television: Among Hispanics—United States," http://en-us.nielsen.com/content/nielsen/en_us/insights/rankings/television.print.html (29 Sept. 2010).

15. *Nielsen Media Research 1992–1993 Report on Television* (New York: Nielsen Media Research, 1993), 9.

16. Mehr, "Women and Ethnic Groups in the Media," 116–18.

17. "TV Usage Greater Among Non-Whites," *Readings in Mass Communication*, edited by Michael Emery and Ted Curtis Smythe (Dubuque, Iowa: Wm. C. Brown Co., 1977), 269.

18. "TV Usage Greater Among Non-Whites," 270–71.

19. *Nielsen Media Research 1992–1993 Report on Television*, 20.

20. *Nielsen Media Research 1992–1993 Report on Television*, 20.

21. *Nielsen Media Research 1992–1993 Report on Television*, 21.

22. *Nielsen Media Research 1992–1993 Report on Television*, 21.

23. "Television, Internet and Mobile Usage in the US: Three Screen Report," The Nielsen Company, Vol. 8, 1st Quarter, 2010, n.p.

24. "Television, Internet and Mobile Usage in the US: Three Screen Report."

25. "Television, Internet and Mobile Usage in the US: Three Screen Report."

26. "Television, Internet and Mobile Usage in the US: Three Screen Report."

27. Debra Gersh, "Promulgating Polarization," *Editor and Publisher* (October 10, 1992), 30.

28. Gersh, "Promulgating Polarization," 30.

29. Mark Fitzgerald, "Covering Crime in Black and White," *Editor and Publisher* (September 10, 1994), 12.

30. Robert M. Entman, "Blacks in the News: Television, Modern Racism and Cultural Change," *Journalism Quarterly* (Summer 1992), 359.

31. Robert M. Entman and Andrew Rojecki, *The Black Image in the White Mind: Media and Race in America* (Chicago: The University of Chicago Press, 2000), 44.

32. Entman and Rojecki, *The Black Image in the White Mind*, 63.

33. Entman and Rojecki, *The Black Image in the White Mind*, 63–64.

34. Clint C. Wilson II, Felix Gutierrez, and Lena M. Chao, *Racism, Sexism and the Media: The Rise of Class Communication in Multicultural America* (Thousand Oaks, Calif.: SAGE Publications, 2003), 117.

35. M. L. Stein, "Relentless Criticism," *Editor and Publisher* (September 4, 1993), 11, 35.

36. Robert Muccigrosso, "Television and the Urban Crisis," *Screen and Society*, edited by Frank J. Coppa (Chicago: Nelson-Hall, 1979), 33.

37. Muccigrosso, "Television and the Urban Crisis," 38.

38. Muccigrosso, "Television and the Urban Crisis," 38–40.

39. Tom Goldstein, ed., *Killing the Messenger: 100 Years of Media Criticism* (New York: Columbia University Press, 1989), 224.

40. Carolyn M. Byerly and Clint C. Wilson II, "Journalism as Kerner Turns 40: Its Multiculticultural Problems and Possibilities," *The Howard Journal of Communications*, 20 (2009), 213.

41. Byerly and Wilson, "Journalism as Kerner Turns 40," 213.

42. William L. Rivers, Wilbur Schramm, and Clifford G. Christians, *Responsibilities in Mass Communication* (New York: Harper and Row, 1980), 209.

43. Bernard Rubin, "See Us, Hear Us, Know Me," *Small Voices and Great Trumpets*, edited by Bernard Rubin (New York: Praeger Publishers, 1980), 5–6.

44. Jeremy Gerard, "Can the Press Do the Right Thing? Hurting Words, Fighting Words," *Columbia Journalism Review* (July/August 1990), 26.

45. Linda Wright Moore, "Can the Press Do the Right Thing? How Your News Looks to Us," *Columbia Journalism Review* (July/August 1990), 23.

46. Rivers, Schramm, and Christians, *Responsibilities in Mass Communication*, 212–13.

47. Rubin, "See Us, Hear Us, Know Me," 6.

48. Mercedes Lynn de Uriarte, "A Problematic Press: Latinos and the News," *Journalism across Cultures*, edited by Fritz Cropp, Cynthia M. Frisby, and Dean Mills (Ames: Iowa State Press, 2003), 57.

49. Rubin, "See Us, Hear Us, Know Me," 6–7.

50. Stanley and Steinberg, *The Media Environment*, 245.

51. Stanley and Steinberg, *The Media Environment*, 246–47.

52. Joe Flint, "Minorities See an Indifferent FCC," *Broadcasting* (August 24, 1992), 25.

53. Joe Flint, "Minorities See an Indifferent FCC," 25.

54. Byerly and Wilson, "Journalism as Kerner Turns 40," 214.

55. Rubin, "See Us, Hear Us, Know Me," 8.

56. Matthew S. Scott, "Can Black Radio Survive an Industry Shakeout?" *Black Enterprise* (June 1993), 255–56.

57. Scott, "Can Black Radio Survive an Industry Shakeout?" 256.

58. Felix Gutierrez, "Chicanos and the Media," *Readings in Mass Communication*, edited by Michael Emery and Ted Curtis Smythe (Dubuque, Iowa: Wm. C. Brown Co., 1977), 290.

59. Gutierrez, "Chicanos and the Media," 290–91.

60. Gutierrez, "Chicanos and the Media," 292.

61. Rubin, "See Us, Hear Us, Know Me," 18.

62. Rubin, "See Us, Hear Us, Know Me," 29.

63. Jim Willis, *Journalism: State of the Art* (Westport, Conn.: Praeger Publishers, 1990), 20.

64. Willis, *Journalism*, 20.

The History and Questionable Quality of Journalism Education

This chapter discusses the history as well as the questionable quality of journalism education. It also comments about accreditation by the Accrediting Council on Education in Journalism and Mass Communications.

In reference to the questionable quality of journalism education the term *quality* differs in meaning. To editors and other professionals in the field, quality means that a student emphasizing journalism has a broad liberal arts background, including courses in history, political science, economics, sociology, literature, and English composition. To educators, quality means that a student has a background in journalism and the liberal arts. These definitions are the author's. The discussion includes criticism by professional members of the media and by journalism educators. General comments are included as well. Specific studies pertaining to journalism education are examined as well.

THE HISTORY OF JOURNALISM EDUCATION IN THE UNITED STATES

In the United States, journalism education was introduced, according to Betty Medsger, "to accomplish two interrelated goals: to improve the minds of journalists and to improve the image of journalism."[1] According to Joseph A. Mirando, "The history of journalism education in America has been shaped by its constant struggle for credibility."[2]

Journalism education started in the 1800s, after the American Civil War. Although one or more individuals had the desire to establish a program that would educate future journalists prior to the war, they were not successful. Furthermore, colleges and universities were for individuals who desired a classical education—that is, understanding one or more classical languages such as Greek, Hebrew, or Latin as well as logic, philosophy, and mathematics, among other established subjects. If students desired to become lawyers, ministers, or physicians, they could enroll in courses that prepared them for those professions. Nonetheless, in 1834, Duff Green, editor of the *United States Telegraph*, announced his intentions of establishing the Washington Institute where students would learn liberal arts and work in his print shop. Green dismissed the idea about the institute, however.[3] In 1857, members of the Board of Directors of the Farmers' High School (now Pennsylvania State University) recommended to the state legislature that journalism become part of the institution's curriculum.[4] However, no courses in journalism were offered until years later.

Perhaps the most influential person responsible for initiating journalism education at a college was General Robert E. Lee who had become president of Washington College (now Washington and Lee University) in Virginia. Lee had served in the Confederate Army during the Civil War. When the war ended in 1865, he accepted the position at Washington College. Lee realized that the Civil War had taken its toll on the South and that the South needed rehabilitation in order to survive. As De Forest O'Dell wrote, "Changes were taking place in other colleges in the South, and a definite attempt was being made to align the educational institutions with the specific problems of reconstruction."[5] Lee also realized that journalism education might help young men of the South find jobs. He realized, too, that society was not necessarily favorable toward the penny press and what it offered the reader. Lee thought that society needed a press that exhibited more responsibility and restraint. As O'Dell wrote, "It was only natural, in view of the examples at hand, for education to be chosen as society's means of control over a rebellious organism."[6] In short, the notion for a curriculum in journalism to be offered by an institution of higher learning was influenced partly by the various reform movements that permeated the country in the 1800s and generally improved social conditions for specific groups if not the entire population. These movements addressed such issues as women's rights, workers' rights, pacifism, and abolitionism, among other causes and issues. As president, Lee had helped build the college by introducing new departments and professional schools, including law and equity as well as civil and mining engineering. He requested that the board of trustees allow instruction in journalism to be offered by the institution. When he proposed a program in journalism, newspapers were published primarily by printers who knew little about editing. Most of these printers were not necessarily considered learned individuals. Most had not attended college, for instance. Indeed, most had learned their occupation on the job or through apprenticeships with other printers. In 1869 Lee introduced the School of Journalism, which had been approved by the board of trustees. Fifty scholarships would be offered to young men who desired to learn how to be editors as well as printers. The proposal for the scholarships had been developed by Professor William Johnson. Unfortunately, only a few scholarships were awarded. The program was covered by the press, however. Unfortunately, many journalists were negative toward the program. A few printers' organizations found the program of interest. Lee died in 1870, and the program in journalism, which had not grown in popularity, died eight years later. It was revived in 1925, however.[7]

After 1870 editors at newspapers and magazines published articles—some pro, most con—about journalism education. For instance, Frederic Hudson, the former managing editor of *The New York Tribune*, wrote,

> Such an establishment as *The New York Herald*, or *Tribune*, or *Times* is the true college for newspaper students. Professor James Gordon Bennett, or Professor Horace Greeley would turn out more real genuine journalists in one year than the Harvards, the Yales, and the Dartmouths could produce in a generation.[8]

Educators were not deterred, however, especially those at the land-grant colleges and universities, which had been established under the provisions of the Morrill Acts of 1862 and 1890. The first bill, which was introduced by Representative Justin Smith Morrill of Vermont and signed into law by President Abraham Lincoln, authorized granting to each state thousands of acres of public land. The law stipulated that the revenue from the sale of these lands had to be used to endow and support at least one college that offered, among other subjects, agriculture and mechanic arts. The second bill provided a federal appropriation to each state for its land-grant college or university.

On April 4, 1872, at New York University, Whitelaw Reid, of the *New York Tribune*, delivered a lecture in which he advocated that journalists should be formally educated. Reid believed that courses in liberal arts should be emphasized more than courses in journalism.[9]

John A. Anderson, president of Kansas State College of Agriculture and Applied Science (now Kansas State University), in 1873 helped establish a course in printing. Later, the Department of Industrial Journalism was founded at the college.

The first president of Cornell University, Andrew Dickson White, provided an outline of a program in journalism that was similar to Whitelaw Reid's. According to White, the program would offer a certificate. Unfortunately, the program was abandoned at Cornell, although lectures in journalism were given in 1876 and one or two courses in journalism were offered by the English Department in 1888.

David Russell McAnally, the head of the School of English at the University of Missouri, introduced journalism to students in 1878. A year later he offered another course in journalism. Occasionally, other courses in journalism were offered by other professors at the university.

During this time, prominent members of the press, including Charles Dana of *The New York Sun*, Joseph Pulitzer of *The New York World*, and Charles Emory Smith of *The Philadelphia Press*, were claiming that the basis of journalism could be taught by competent professors who had practical experience in journalism.

Eugene Camp of the *Philadelphia Times* encouraged the University of Pennsylvania to develop a curriculum in journalism. In 1893, Professor Joseph French Johnson of the university's Wharton School of Business became the director of the newly developed program of professional training for newspaper work, which was the first comprehensive curriculum in journalism offered in the country. Johnson had worked at *The Chicago Tribune*.

Johnson's program consisted of the following:

Journalism—Art and History of Newspaper Making.

Journalism—Law of Libel, Business Management, Typographical Union, Cost and Revenue, Advertising, Method of Criticism, etc.

Journalism—Newspaper Practice, Exercises in Reporting, Editing of Copy, Conversations, etc.

Journalism—Current Topics, Lectures on Live Issues in the United States and Foreign Countries.

Journalism—Public Lectures by Men Engaged in the Active Work of the Profession.[10]

Johnson left his position in 1901 when he was offered a dean's position at New York University.

Dr. E. M. Hopkins, who was chair of the Department of English at the University of Kansas, offered a course in journalism in 1894. No other courses in journalism were offered at this institution, however, until 1903.[11]

During this period other colleges and universities offered one or more courses in journalism, including Temple University, Indiana University, the University of Michigan, and the University of Nebraska, among others.

In 1896 E. W. Stephens, the publisher of the *Columbia Herald*, addressed members of the Missouri Press Association and encouraged them that Missouri and the nation needed programs in journalism. The members responded by adopting a resolution that, in 1898, persuaded the president and the board at the University of Missouri to establish a "Chair of Journalism." Although the university catalog listed a Department of Journalism, it existed only on paper for several years. Courses in journalism had been offered in the School of English for years, however, probably because of Norman Coleman. Coleman, a journalist, in 1869 had suggested that the university offer study in the subject.[12]

In 1898 the board of directors created a School of Journalism at Bessie Tift College in Forsyth, Georgia. The courses varied, but most focused on a specific form of writing. The program was revamped in 1923.

The University of Chicago offered its first course in journalism in 1899. Three years later the College of Commerce and Administration offered a major in journalism, which lasted until 1911.

In 1903 other institutions offered at least one course in journalism. These included the University of North Dakota and Iowa State College of Agriculture and Mechanical Arts (now Iowa State University).

Joseph Pulitzer, who had become an extremely successful publisher and editor and who had desired to endow a school of journalism since 1892, announced in *The New York World*, August 16, 1903, that he had endowed a school of journalism at Columbia University. Pulitzer expressed his position on education for journalism in an article that appeared in the *North American Review*. Pulitzer described a program that focused on (1) style, (2) law tailored for the journalist, (3) ethics, (4) literature, (5) truth and accuracy, (6) history tailored for the journalist, (7) sociology, (8) economics, (9) "the enemies of the republic," (10) arbitration in its broad sense, (11) statistics, (12) modern languages, especially French and German, (13) science, (14) the study of newspapers, (15) the power of ideas, (16) principles of journalism, and (17) the news.[13]

Pulitzer's idea for an endowed school of journalism had been discussed at length in a brochure that had been given to the presidents of Harvard University and Columbia University. The president of Columbia responded positively to Pulitzer's plan. Harvard's president, Dr. Charles W. Eliot, had been off campus. Eventually, he responded, but his curriculum stressed the business side of journalism. Pulitzer was not necessarily interested in Dr. Eliot's proposed curriculum, although it was listed in the *World*. Dr. Eliot's proposal consisted of the following:

1. Newspaper Administration (the organization of a newspaper office and functions of various departments and services).

2. Newspaper Manufacture (study of printing presses and other mechanical devices used in publishing).
3. The Law of Journalism.
4. Ethics of Journalism.
5. History of Journalism.
6. The Literary Forms of Newspapers (approved usages in punctuation, spelling, abbreviations, typography, etc.).[14]

Dr. Eliot's proposal focused on editorial work, operation of the business office, operation of the advertising office, and operation of the mechanical department. He suggested that other departments at the university, including English, history, government, geography, and economics, could offer courses relevant to journalism. In essence, these "background" courses would be coordinated with the journalism program.

Dr. Eliot was also listed in the newspaper as a temporary member of the Advisory Board for the new school of journalism at Columbia. He could not serve as a permanent member because of his position at Harvard, however.

Basically, Pulitzer's plan emphasized a liberal arts education, while Dr. Eliot's plan emphasized practical courses or so-called skills courses. Although some early programs offered courses that were based on Pulitzer's ideas, most early programs offered courses that were based on Dr. Eliot's ideas. Eventually, the curriculum in journalism was broadened; more liberal arts types of courses were offered while skills types of courses were limited.[15]

Pulitzer and the *World*, by including Dr. Eliot and his curriculum in the stories about the endowed new school, brought academic credibility to the new school, which received praise as well as criticism from journalists throughout the country. In 1904 the National Editorial Association announced that it supported Pulitzer and his endowment. Pulitzer died in 1911, and the building housing the new school was finished in 1913. The first few courses had been offered in 1912. Columbia's School of Journalism offered courses to undergraduates for years. In 1931, however, the school changed its focus. Only students who had earned bachelor's degrees would be considered for admission to the new graduate program.

Journalism developed at the University of Illinois in the early 1900s. In 1905 Dr. Frank Scott developed the first four-year curriculum in journalism at the university. His curriculum was influenced by Pulitzer and Dr. Eliot at Harvard.

Dr. Willard G. Bleyer introduced journalism on the campus of the University of Wisconsin in 1905. The course was offered initially in the English Department. Bleyer was influenced by Pulitzer, Dr. Eliot, and his own formal education. Bleyer basically agreed with Pulitzer in that he thought a program in journalism could help students understand the role of the press in society or how the press had impacted society, especially democracy. He also believed that students should learn the skills of journalism as well as how journalism had been practiced. More courses in journalism were added to the curriculum, which became part of a two-year program. In 1912 a department was created. Bleyer was one of the first educators to help develop a graduate program in journalism.

Without question, Dr. Eliot's proposed curriculum was the basis for the first school of journalism, which was founded in 1908 at the University of Missouri. The School of Journalism offered an undergraduate program that focused on practical skills such as writing and editing. In essence, the program's purpose was to prepare students for the profession. The School of Journalism's curriculum was copied by other universities.

Sigma Delta Chi, the Society of Professional Journalists, was founded at DePauw University in 1909. Pi Delta Epsilon, the Society for Collegiate Journalists, was founded at Syracuse University the same year. Kappa Tau Alpha, the national honors society for journalism students, was founded at the University of Missouri in 1910. These organizations provided students who emphasized journalism additional opportunities and recognition.

An editorial in the *Journalism Bulletin* claimed that one school and three departments of journalism existed by 1910. These included the school at the University of Missouri and departments at the Universities of Wisconsin, New York, and Washington. The editorial also claimed that one or more courses in journalism were offered at the following colleges and universities: Bessie Tift College, Cornell University, DePauw University, Indiana University, Kansas State College of Agriculture and Applied Science, Ohio University, University of Colorado, University of Illinois, University of Michigan, University of Nebraska, University of North Dakota, University of Oklahoma, and University of Pennsylvania.[16]

Journalism education grew in popularity. In 1912, for instance, based on a report by Walter Williams, dean of the School of Journalism at the University of Missouri, thirty-two institutions were offering courses in journalism. Three of the institutions had professional schools of journalism while seven others had departments of journalism.[17]

According to James Melvin Lee, there were ninety-one institutions offering courses in journalism by 1918. The number of institutions offering courses in journalism had increased to 131 by 1920.[18]

In the 1920s other publishers and editors of newspapers as well as professional organizations encouraged colleges and universities to establish programs in journalism. In 1921, for example, Joseph Medill Patterson and Robert Mc-Cormick of the *Chicago Tribune* supported the founding of the Medill School of Journalism at Northwestern University. William J. Murphy of the *Minneapolis Tribune* provided funding for a school of journalism at the University of Minnesota in 1924. The New Jersey Press Association helped establish a journalism department at Rutgers University in 1925. The *Times-Picayune* of New Orleans funded a chair of journalism at Tulane University in 1927.

The number of institutions offering courses in journalism increased every year. In 1932, for instance, there were 326 institutions offering courses in journalism. Two years later there were 455 institutions.[19]

As more relationships between newspaper publishers and colleges and universities were established, the journalism programs focused more on practical skills courses and less on courses that would help students improve the profession and subsequently society. Consequently, college and university administrators reacted by encouraging faculty who taught journalism to hire colleagues with doctorates. These administrators realized that journalism programs were becoming nothing more than trade schools or vocational schools primarily because of the curriculum's emphasis on skills.

The American Association of Teachers of Journalism reacted in 1935 by adopting a statement that basically objected to administrators' wishes. Members of this organization believed that the doctorate was not as important as professional experience. Unfortunately, this action exhibited how faculty who taught journalism believed. As a result, administrators and faculty in other academic disciplines criticized programs in journalism for not being rigorous and for not having the same academic requirements for faculty as other disciplines. On the other hand, many journalism programs were recognized by publishers and editors at newspapers for producing graduates who knew enough to be hired.

In 1936, during the Great Depression, there were 532 institutions offering courses in journalism. There were 542 institutions—more than 60 percent of the country's four-year, degree-granting colleges and universities—offering courses in journalism before 1940. Only 103 of these institutions offered a major in journalism, however.[20]

Administrators and faculty in other academic disciplines continued to criticize journalism education. Of course, they had very good reasons. In 1938 Vernon Nash claimed that college and university administrators had approved courses in journalism that required students to write publicity articles about the institutions and nothing else.[21] In 1939 fewer than fifty of the country's one thousand college and university faculty members who taught journalism had earned a doctorate; more than one hundred had no college degree whatsoever.[22] These numbers indicated that most, if not all, of the journalism programs were inferior when compared to other academic disciplines.

To make matters worse, in 1945 Albert Sutton found that most journalism programs had no laboratory facilities for students or library holdings in journalism.[23] Of course, there were a few exceptions. These few programs were on the campuses of major state universities. A few of these programs were addressing change perhaps as a result of criticism by journalists and notable educators, perhaps as a result of interest on the part of some who were teaching courses in journalism. These educators, in addition to studying and writing about journalism, also examined what became known as communication studies and mass communication, which eventually broadened the curriculum at numerous programs. Eventually, some scholars began teaching courses that were closely related to behavioral science. As Norval Neil Luxon wrote,

> Professional education for journalism has come of age. . . . It has joined the social and behavioral sciences in a broad study of communications in modern society, and in so doing it simultaneously is providing better training for tomorrow's editors and publishers.[24]

Dr. Willard Bleyer was partly responsible for the mass communication or social science approach to journalism education. In 1929 he helped develop a doctoral program at the University of Wisconsin in which students majored in a social science area and earned a minor in journalism. Some of the exceptional students became directors and deans at other journalism programs and subsequently encouraged their faculties to broaden their curriculums to include courses in mass communications. This occurred at several universities, including the University of Minnesota.

In 1944 the University of Minnesota's School of Journalism established a division of research. A few other large schools that had some faculty with doctorates and graduate programs followed the University of Minnesota's lead, especially in the 1950s. These research divisions allowed primarily senior faculty with doctorates to conduct research about areas other than journalism. Indeed, research by these faculty members concerned communication and its effects on people, among other topics. Some of this research brought some recognition and, more important, some respectability to the faculty members' programs. Research also allowed senior faculty the opportunity to teach graduate courses instead of undergraduate skills courses.

As a result of more divisions of research being founded, universities needed faculty who knew how to conduct it. Consequently, faculty members with doctorates were desired, especially by faculty and administrators at large programs that offered undergraduate and graduate degrees.

Dr. Wilbur Schramm, who was similar to Dr. Bleyer in that he had a doctorate in English and little journalism experience, was interested in mass communication research. Although he has been credited for strengthening programs and research centers at the University of Iowa, the University of Illinois, Stanford University, and the University of Hawaii, he was responsible, perhaps more than any other scholar, for communication studies becoming part of journalism programs. (Some scholars claim that communication studies have taken over so-called journalism programs and consequently the programs' missions.) Of course, some would argue that Dr. Schramm did not take journalism seriously. To him, the subject was not intellectually challenging or stimulating. Dr. Schramm developed institutes of communication studies and doctoral degree-granting programs in mass communications. These programs produced scholars who became interested in conducting research about communication studies, not necessarily journalism.[25] Much of this research was sociological and qualitative in nature. Much of this research paled when compared to research generated by scholars in other academic disciplines. Everett Rogers claimed that these scholars had little concern about how journalism education would be impacted.[26]

Although the School of Journalism at the University of Missouri offered the first Ph.D. degree in 1934, the graduate program did not confer another doctorate until 1940. In short, doctoral education in journalism was not popular. In addition, it was sporadic at the few institutions that eventually had doctoral programs. Only eight doctoral programs existed from the late 1940s until 1966. By 1975 there were twenty programs. By 1988 there were thirty-one programs.[27]

As more journalism programs desired faculty with doctorates, the expectation of faculty having professional journalism experience decreased. Concurrently, practicing journalists criticized programs in journalism for hiring people with doctorates instead of people with professional journalism experience.

Criticism aside, newspaper publishers and editors hired graduates. Enrollments at journalism programs grew. In 1960, for instance, there were 11,000 students. In 1970 there were 33,000 students.[28] There were several reasons for such growth. One was the Vietnam War. Young people, especially young men, were drafted if they were not attending colleges or universities. Consequently, many young people sought security on college and university campuses. Another reason was that the baby boomers were encouraged to continue their education. Their parents had experienced the Great Depression or had learned about it from their parents. Certainly, they did not want their children to suffer like they had, and a college education quite possibly could prevent hardship or at least a job that few enjoyed. Another reason was the curriculum. In many journalism programs the curriculum consisted of numerous skills courses. These courses were generally easier and more practical than, say, courses in literature, philosophy, history, and other subjects that required a lot of reading and critical thinking. Of course, another reason was perhaps the popularity of Bob Woodward and Carl Bernstein, who together investigated the Watergate break-in and wrote about it as well as its impact on the president of the United States. President Richard Nixon eventually resigned in disgrace.

In 1970 about one-half of all colleges and universities in the United States offered a course in journalism. About one-fifth offered a major in journalism.[29] Enrollments continued to increase. Indeed, journalism programs attracted some 140,000 students in 1988.[30] There were more than 200,000 students in 2008, a number that is staggering, considering that the industry has witnessed fewer readers and has let go thousands of workers. Radio and television stations, too, have been impacted by the newer technology, which has appealed to people. Specific radio personalities as well as certain television programs have experienced fewer listeners and viewers.

Change continued, however. As more faculty members with doctorates filled positions, the emphasis on journalism decreased. Most doctoral programs focused on communication studies or mass communications, not journalism. Fortunately or unfortunately, depending on one's perspective, this area of emphasis has trickled down to the undergraduate curriculum. Indeed, undergraduate courses in communication studies and mass communications were developed by faculty members and approved by college and university committees. These courses were then added to the curriculum. In some instances, these courses replaced journalism courses.

Still, the primary purpose of many journalism programs is to offer students enough practical courses so they will be prepared for entry-level positions in one or several of the mass media. Of course, there are professors in journalism programs who make certain that students understand how the media function in society as well as how the media can be improved. However, these professors usually are scholars and do not necessarily teach at the undergraduate level, unless they are obligated to. Rather, they teach courses at the graduate level that they believe encourage students to question the media and its role in society. Generally, these courses are more about communication studies and mass communications than about journalism. On the other hand, there are programs that emphasize journalism, but these programs are in the minority, not the majority, primarily because of the teaching and research interests of the faculty. Many programs include disciplines such as advertising and public relations in addition to journalism. Even so-called journalism faculty members tend to be interested in communication studies or mass communications, not necessarily journalism. As a result of these changes there is much confusion in journalism education.

A BRIEF HISTORY OF ACADEMIC ORGANIZATIONS IN JOURNALISM

The first academic organization for professors of journalism was the American Association of Teachers of Journalism (AATJ), which Dr. Willard Bleyer helped found in 1912. This organization founded the Committee on Research in 1924, which published the organization's first journal, *Journalism Bulletin*, the same year. Dr. Lawrence Murphy of the University of North Dakota was the first editor. The American Association of Teachers of Journalism became the Association for Education in Journalism (AEJ) in 1950. In 1964 the organization approved special interest divisions and elected standing committees. These divisions represented members' interests such as research, standards of teaching, and professional freedom and responsibility. A year later the organization approved more divisions that were based on members' disciplines such as advertising, communication theory and methodology, graphic arts, history, international communication, magazine, newspaper, public relations, radio-television journalism, and secondary education. The organization changed its name to the Association for Education in Journalism and Mass Communication (AEJMC) in 1982 primarily to reflect the broad curriculum of the typical school or department of journalism, communication, or mass communications ("journalism" was replaced with "communication" or "mass communications" at numerous schools or departments as the programs' areas of concentrations grew).[31]

The American Association of Schools and Departments of Journalism (AASDJ) was founded in 1917. Dr. Bleyer helped found this organization as well. In order for a school or department to become a member of this organization, the program had to offer mostly skills courses in journalism, including reporting, writing, and editing. The American Association of Schools and Departments of Journalism organized a Council on Education in Journalism in 1923. The purpose of this body was to develop and maintain standards of journalistic education. The "Principles and Standards of Education for

Journalism," which the council developed, expressed educators' views about journalism education. The educators believed in a solid liberal arts foundation. The "Principles and Standards of Education for Journalism" were adopted by the American Association of Schools and Departments of Journalism and the American Association of Teachers of Journalism in 1924. The principles were revised more than once over the years and approved by the American Association of Schools and Departments of Journalism. Such work continued in this organization and the American Association of Teachers of Journalism, which met annually. Both organizations, along with the professional organization, the American Society of Newspaper Editors, organized a joint committee that was composed of members from various national organizations, including the American Association of Schools and Departments of Journalism, the American Association of Teachers of Journalism, the American Society of Newspaper Editors, and the National Editorial Association. Other professional groups became involved by 1939, and the National Council on Professional Education for Journalism was established primarily to identify the problems of journalism education and, of course, raise the standards of instruction in the field.

The American Association of Schools and Departments of Journalism merged with the American Society of Journalism School Administrators (AS-JSA), which had been founded in 1945, to form the Association of Schools of Journalism and Mass Communication (ASJMC) in 1984. The American Society of Journalism School Administrators had disagreed over accrediting procedures by the American Council on Education in Journalism (ACEJ), which had been founded in 1945, and the American Association of Schools and Departments of Journalism.

Accreditation of journalism programs by the American Council on Education in Journalism began in 1945. The accrediting body applied the controversial "75-25" rule in its evaluations of programs. This meant that the typical graduate of an accredited journalism program had enrolled in mostly liberal arts courses (75 percent of all courses required for the bachelor's degree had to be in liberal arts). Only 25 percent of all courses required had been in journalism. This ratio was widely accepted by journalism educators before 1950. The American Council on Education in Journalism changed its name to the Accrediting Council on Education in Journalism and Mass Communications (ACEJMC) in 1980. The controversial ratio of 75 percent of a student's total courses in liberal arts and 25 percent in journalism was replaced in 1989 with the "90-65" rule, which meant that 90 hours of the typical 120 hours required for the bachelor's degree had to be in courses outside the major and 65 of these hours had to be in liberal arts.[32]

CRITICISM OF JOURNALISM EDUCATION

Criticism of journalism education has existed since the late 1800s. Such criticism appeared when college administrators first thought about offering courses in journalism. For instance, Paul Dressel pointed out, "Though there was general agreement that the newspaperman should be well educated, the prevalent view rejected a formal curriculum in favor of learning by experience on one of the better papers of the day."[33] Nonetheless, education in journalism developed. However, between the late 1800s and 1925 journalism programs were mere trade schools. Vocational education was the norm, to say the least. Respect toward journalism education by faculty members in other disciplines—that is, if they have ever had respect for journalism education—came many years later. Charles Wingate, who wrote for different newspapers, published *Views and Interviews on Journalism* in 1875. This book contained numerous interviews with various journalists as well as articles about journalism. Some of the book's content pertained to journalism education. For example, he asked Henry Waterson, editor of the *Louisville Courier-Journal*, about newspaper training. Waterson responded,

> There is but one school of journalism and that is a well-conducted newspaper office. To be sure, this may be preceded by a certain special course of study in political economy and belles-lettres. But versatility of talent and accomplishment—which, as a rule, is a drawback—is in journalism a prime necessity, and this cannot be acquired within the narrow compass of an editorial college. I don't believe a journalist can be made to order.[34]

Wingate asked Horace White of *The Chicago Tribune*, Frederic Hudson of *The New York Tribune*, and E. L. Godkin of *The Nation*, among other prominent journalists, similar questions. Most agreed with Waterson. In essence, there was only one place where journalism could be learned and that was in a respectable newspaper or magazine office.

Gardner Cowles, Jr., an editor, criticized journalism education as well in 1928. He claimed that it limited the imagination because it emphasized practical instruction. According to Cowles, journalism education placed "too much stress on routine work on the college daily. He called for greater emphasis on broad principles and problems of editing."[35]

In 1930 Abraham Flexner said journalism education was "on a par with university faculties of cookery and clothing."[36] Flexner condemned the programs at Columbia University and the University of Wisconsin because of their vocational orientation. The same year the American Society of Newspaper Editors claimed that skills could be taught in newspaper offices. The organization recommended that the journalism curriculum become mostly a liberal arts education and that schools of journalism become graduate schools comparable to those of law and medicine.[37]

In 1938 Robert Maynard Hutchins severely criticized journalism education. He characterized schools of journalism as "the shadiest education ventures under respectable auspices."[38]

In 1947 the Commission on Freedom of the Press, which Hutchins chaired, reported:

> Most [journalism schools] devote themselves to vocational training, and even here they are not so effective as they should be. The kind of training a journalist needs most today is not training in the tricks and machinery of the trade. If he is to be a competent judge of public affairs, he needs the broadest and most liberal education. The schools of journalism as a whole have not yet successfully worked out the method by which their students may acquire this education.[39]

As a result of such criticism, the liberal arts curriculum was (and is) emphasized by the Accrediting Council on Education in Journalism and Mass Communications (ACEJMC). Indeed, today the ACEJMC recommends that a student emphasizing journalism earn at least sixty-five hours in liberal arts, such as English, political science, history, sociology, psychology, science, and mathematics. Of course, this author believes that this requirement prohibits students from enrolling in other important subjects such as those found in business programs.

Fortunately, criticism of journalism education continued. *Fortunately* is used because journalism—like any discipline—needs criticism in order to change. Since education should evolve, change is necessary.

In 1963 and 1964, in two articles appropriately titled "What's Happening to Journalism Education?" John Tebbel caused practitioners to applaud and educators to squirm in their chairs. Among Tebbel's criticisms were:

1. Certain professors have stopped reading newspapers.
2. Certain professors have forgotten their purpose: to train individuals to interpret thoughtfully today's complicated information and to communicate information effectively.
3. Research has replaced teaching in graduate programs in the largest schools.
4. Emphasis on research has caused a de-emphasis of the professional curriculum. Indeed, certain research faculty members do not have any professional media experience.[40]

It must be remembered that a university's prestige is measured in one sense by the number of faculty with doctorates. Since a university's administration deems research as one of its missions, the quest for faculty with doctorates will not cease. On the contrary, the quest will grow stronger. (It should be mentioned that one of the reasons journalism education has been criticized by college and university administrators as well as faculty members in other disciplines is because of its history of hiring people who did not have the appropriate academic credentials such as the doctorate. As mentioned, people without college degrees have been hired by journalism programs.) However, Tebbel's point about faculty with little or no professional experience must seriously be considered by both administrators and journalism faculty.

In 1965 David Boroff provided other criticisms. In his article, "What Ails the Journalism Schools?" which was based on a study for the Ford Foundation, he pointed out,

1. Certain journalism faculty members are failed reporters.
2. The Ph.D. "has the effect of freezing out some of the best journalist-teachers."
3. About 50 percent of the journalism programs do not support the university's newspaper.[41]

Boroff believed that journalism programs needed to hire journalists who could teach instead of those who had Ph.D.s. He also believed that a journalism program needed to have its students work for the university's newspaper, primarily because they could practice their skills and learn about freedom of the press and responsibility.[42]

Regarding Boroff's first point, one has to speculate that what he claimed is true. His second point, on the other hand, is based solidly on fact. Some of the best instructors perhaps are kept out of journalism programs because they do not meet the requirements, specifically the Ph.D. or some other doctoral degree. However, research is deemed important by college and university administrators as well as faculty members at prestigious institutions. (Considering that college and university budgets have been slashed, faculty who can do research, especially research that brings in dollars from external entities as well as research that garners national or international recognition, will be considered by hiring committees to fill positions. Of course, hiring committees need to consider faculty who can write books for a scholarly audience. Books, particularly those that are reviewed favorably in respected journals, often generate more discussion about a program in journalism than academic articles based on research.) Boroff's third point, although possibly true at the time he wrote the article, is not true today. Most schools of journalism are involved directly or indirectly in student publications. Many of these publications have online versions.

In 1971 M. L. Stein (then chairman of the Department of Journalism at New York University) pointed out similar arguments:

1. Should the curriculum focus on the practical courses in reporting or on the social effects of the mass media? Should reporters or the behavioral scientists manage journalism programs?
2. Hostility exists between older faculty with professional media experience and young faculty with Ph.D.s who have little, if any, professional media experience and who are indifferent to skills courses.
3. Research faculty influence and perhaps dominate the Association for Education in Journalism and Mass Communications.
4. The older faculty with professional media experience sneer at the research studies conducted by the younger faculty with Ph.D.s. The older faculty claim that the emphasis on research diverts journalism programs from their primary purpose: to educate people for the nation's print and broadcast media.
5. The older faculty with media experience believe that the younger faculty with Ph.D.s have an anti-media bias.[43]

Stein's comments are relevant to today's journalism programs. There seems to be two camps, as he mentioned. And the researchers do not like to teach the "trivial" courses—that is, the skills courses, such as writing, editing, and such. As far as the Association for Education in Journalism and Mass Communications is concerned, researchers do hold a considerable amount of power. However, one must remember that the profession itself has more power than it had in the past. If newspaper publishers and editors are not happy with the people they hire, they can either fire those individuals or not hire others who have graduated from particular colleges and universities. The same can be stated for those who are responsible for employing people at radio and television stations. Or the publishers or editors can contact specific colleges and universities and comment on the quality of education. Most department heads or deans will listen. After all, if a specific program earns a poor reputation, students may be encouraged by others to go elsewhere. Although magazines such as *U.S. News & World Report* identify so-called excellent programs in various disciplines at colleges and universities, these magazines seldom identify programs in journalism. This is not to state that other sources have not. For instance, at least one annual publication published by Peterson's identified the so-called better journalism programs. Prior to this *The Gourman Report* ranked the best programs.

It is difficult to assess the truth of Stein's comment about faculty who have Ph.D.s bringing with them an anti-media bias. Nonetheless, such a statement should not be taken lightly. It may contain an ounce of truth.

In 1972, at a symposium on "Education for Newspaper Work" cosponsored by the Southern Newspaper Publishers Association Foundation and the University of South Carolina, editors pointed out "that journalism schools frequently do not take advantage of available opportunities to have professionals visit, nor do they go to the newspapers to learn themselves what is happening there."[44]

The editors and educators agreed that students who graduated from journalism programs had a weak command of the English language.

These points must be considered. Apparently many professionals believe the same because several complaints keep appearing. Whether instructors of journalism can actually improve students' ability to write in one to three courses is debatable. After all, most students who attend college have had three or four years of high school English. If they have not learned how to write by the time they graduate from high school, how can publishers and editors expect a journalism professor to teach students the fundamentals of writing in one to three classes? Perhaps their expectations are too high or unrealistic. Or their criticism is misplaced. Of course, programs in journalism should require students to pass entrance tests that measure students' ability to write before they are accepted to study journalism. Programs in journalism should also require students to have higher grade point averages (say, a 3.0 based on a 4.0 scale) based on thirty or forty-five hours of academic credit before the students are accepted to study journalism.

In 1973, at a conference sponsored by the American Newspaper Publishers Association Foundation and the Association for Education in Journalism and Mass Communications, editors and educators pointed out the following criticism:

> Too many non-journalism introductory courses are geared to lead toward advanced, graduate work and not to provide the real, basic nuts-and-bolts needed by newsmen. If this problem cannot otherwise be solved, most administrators agreed that the journalism school or department should offer its own program in the area.[45]

In 1974, at a symposium on "Education for Newspaper Careers . . . Satisfied?" sponsored by the Western Newspaper Foundation, all publishers present agreed that journalism schools were doing a poor job. The keynote speaker, Ronald H. Einstoss, pointed out,

1. Many applicants "lack a working knowledge of English."
2. Many applicants are being taught that a lead contains the five Ws and an H. They are not taught that a reader's degree of understanding drops significantly after twenty words.
3. Many applicants do not have a background in liberal arts and the sciences. "They know little of local government."[46]

Specific criticisms that were mentioned before are mentioned above. Unfortunately, numerous journalism programs have an open door policy—that is, many programs allow every student who applies in, no matter what their writing ability is. Only the programs that have entrance examinations can deny students who have writing deficiencies. Instead of having an open door policy, all journalism programs should require a certain score on an entrance examination, as mentioned. Students who do not do well should not be allowed to emphasize journalism. Of course, college and university administrators may grow concerned about enrollment figures, but enrollment figures need to be lower anyway. There are too many students majoring in journalism.

In the November/December 1974 issue of the American Society of Newspaper Editors *Bulletin*, Ted Bush reported the following "basic gripes" that editors have toward journalism graduates and journalism programs:

1. They are weak in English grammar, punctuation, and spelling.
2. Faculties may not know what newsrooms are doing.
3. Faculty salaries need to be increased; such would appeal to outstanding professionals who may desire to teach and would eliminate "cheap labor"— those who failed as reporters.
4. Faculties are loaded with Ph.D.s who are interested in research more than they are in teaching.
5. Faculties should not have to write for scholarly journals in order to be eligible for promotion.
6. Class size, particularly in writing courses, should be limited.[47]

Although Bush's "basic gripes" include most of the complaints previously mentioned, several new ones appear. The suggestion for higher pay is an example. However, in order to raise salaries of most educators of journalism, every journalism school would have to receive additional funding. Where would the money come from? The public? Private corporations? The media? If funding came from the public, whether at the local, state, or national level, academia probably would be criticized by specific groups within the public sector. Besides, students' tuitions and fees have increased substantially over the past few years; consequently, parents should not be asked to pay more. Higher education is not the nation's highest priority. This may be unfortunate, considering that a student who graduates from a college or university will earn considerably more on average than someone who does not. Of course, this college or university graduate will pay on average more taxes. Gifts from private corporations, specifically corporations that own newspapers, radio stations, television stations, magazines, and other media, have been given from time to time. Unfortunately, such funding, in most cases, has allowed a certain school of journalism to hire perhaps one or two distinguished professionals or purchase equipment for a laboratory. This practice has at least two drawbacks: the professionals are usually hired for either one or two years, and only the elite state-supported or private schools of journalism receive any contributions of any consequence. The small state-supported and private schools seldom receive such gifts.

In the Autumn–Winter 1975 issue of *Nieman Reports*, Ronald Farrar pointed out the following problems with journalism education:

1. Too many students; too few qualified faculty members.
2. Too many graduates; too few jobs.
3. Students lack motivation.
4. Technology is expensive for certain programs in journalism.
5. Quality of faculty is uneven. "Ideally, the journalism professor should bring to his position several years of worthwhile experience as a working journalist as well as appropriate academic credentials."[48]

Farrar's assertions must be considered. Indeed, there are too many students enrolled in journalism, too few qualified instructors to teach the required courses, too few instructors with sufficient experience, and not enough funds to pay for the costly but necessary equipment. There are solutions, however. As mentioned, students should be required to pass an entrance examination in order to be accepted into a journalism program. Only students who pass the examination should be admitted. These students will be motivated more than likely or they would not have taken an examination and passed it in order to be admitted to a particular program. Faculty hired should be qualified for the courses that are assigned to them. Technology is expensive, and excellent journalism programs have the necessary equipment to help students learn. If colleges and universities do not have technology fees that students have to pay, then such should be implemented. Such fees can be paid when other fees are paid by students. Or the college or university can request funding from foundations that represent specific media companies. Of course, not every foundation will provide funds for purchasing equipment.

Ben Bagdikian, in his "Woodstein U" article, which was published in 1977 in the *Atlantic*, caused journalism educators to write to the magazine for several months. Apparently, some of what Bagdikian stated hit some nerves. For instance, in discussing one of the largest journalism schools in the nation, the University of Texas at Austin, he pointed out that many of the faculty who taught journalism had graduated from the university and had worked for papers in Texas. He wrote, "Forty percent of all new reporters for Texas papers come from the school. But the faculty is not distinctive in either the practice of journalism or journalistic research."[49]

Bagdikian mentioned that the education of journalists was "fairly rigorous and realistic" in "some of the better undergraduate" as well as in the graduate programs. However, he added that "the level of training drops precipitously at the easy going colleges and at most junior colleges."[50]

Bagdikian claimed that those who hire students who majored in journalism "have mixed but largely negative attitudes toward the value of journalism education."[51]

Bagdikian's complaints concerning the large journalism schools, specifically the University of Texas at Austin, have been remedied, for the most part, by discerning administrators. The problems confronting junior colleges, however, are another story. One problem is keeping faculty who have strong qualifications to teach journalism. Generally, these people do not stay at junior or community colleges long, especially if they desire to teach at a four-year college or university. Another problem is that many of these two-year institutions do not have the necessary resources or the proper equipment on which students can be trained. For example, few community colleges can afford to invest every few years in new computers and other hardware that are needed for laboratories. Yet, such is important today. Of course, if these colleges have enacted fees that are charged to students, then this problem may not exist.

In 1977, Mal Deans reported "that about two-thirds of American schools and departments of journalism, of which there are about 250, now have some sort of electronic equipment."[52]

He pointed out,

> The electronic age, however, has created some problems for journalism teachers. Many educators, and editors as well, have expressed concern that fascination with the new technology may result in de-emphasis of the basics—teaching students how to report, write and edit properly.[53]

This assertion has been shown to be true. Indeed, students appear to be interested in learning how to operate a particular software program rather than learning certain principles or theoretical concepts.

Darrell Berkheimer, then news editor at the *Provo Daily Herald*, wrote in 1979 that "the university should be placing more emphasis on finding an instructor with a solid 15 to 30 years experience in business, and forget about the master's degree requirement."[54]

He criticized journalism schools' instructors for presenting the "wrongful" emphasis on "investigative reporting":

> Somehow, many beginning reporters are coming out of J-schools with super-liberal ideas and ambitions on how they will become "investigative" reporters and columnists. And they have the idea that the use of a byline allows them to "interpret" the news as they see fit, using the facts as they choose them.[55]

Berkheimer has a point. There was a time when a course in journalistic ethics was required of every student majoring in journalism. This is not true today. Not every journalism school requires every student who majors in journalism to enroll in its ethics course.

Creed Black, then chairman and publisher of the Lexington, Kentucky *Herald-Leader*, in 1979 wrote that he read *Journalism Quarterly* (now *Journalism and Mass Communication Quarterly*), hoping to find articles of value. However, because he found little he could understand or apply, he concluded that his reading time "would be more productively spent on English-language publications."[56]

Black admitted that there was a place for research in journalism schools, "but it should be directed to the problems that actually confront working journalists and should be reported in terms that a reasonably intelligent editor or publisher can understand."[57]

Black and other publishers and editors like him must admit that some research is useful and simple to understand. For example, studies that seek to determine what may prejudice jurors or studies that illustrate the deficiencies in coverage of the elderly or other groups have merit. Much research done for various press groups—whether national, state, or local—has merit. Indeed, such can contribute to media performance and, concurrently, dispel people's erroneous beliefs and confirm their correct beliefs. For example, studies that determine what the majority of people think about a specific issue or political candidate are generally interesting to editors and audiences alike. Several journalism programs have established research centers that allow faculty members to conduct research that is newsworthy. This research is published frequently in newspapers and broadcast on local television news programs. Occasionally, it is published in nationally circulated newspapers and broadcast on major network news programs. However, more journalism programs should be encouraged to open research centers that allow faculty to conduct research that will interest news organizations. Of course, these centers should encourage faculty to conduct academic research suitable for refereed national and international conferences, conference proceedings, and scholarly journals, too.

In his article, "What's Wrong with Journalism Education?" published in 1980, Warren Schwed, a former employee of UPI, McGraw-Hill, and *Newsweek*, pointed out that there were several problems with journalism education. One was the "teachers." According to Schwed, "Many lack relevant professional experience for teaching skills courses like reporting, writing, [and] editing."[58]

Schwed also mentioned that salaries were too low to attract people who had professional media experience. Regarding what should be taught, Schwed mentioned that people who had professional media experience stressed skills courses—that is, reporting, writing, editing, and law. Those who did not have professional media experience stressed theory courses.[59]

Regarding journalism students, Schwed pointed out that the students could not spell, punctuate, or write. In addition, they rarely read.[60]

Schwed mentioned that instructors could make it tough on students, but few did because of survival—that is, they were evaluated by students and they enjoyed being liked by students. Also, administrators preferred faculty to pass along weak and borderline students.[61]

Schwed mentioned several points that others have discussed. However, his last point must be considered. Usually the practice of passing along weak students is for a simple reason: numbers often affect budget appropriations. The more students an institution has generally means the more funding it will receive. This is true generally for colleges and departments within the institution as well. Therefore, a college or department within an institution cannot afford to fail too many students, some administrators rationalize. Of course, instead of funding departments, colleges, and institutions based on enrollment, another formula for funding should be developed. For instance, should every state institution have the same academic programs? Of course not. Because journalism is not a discipline like English, which is a required subject at most, if not all, institutions, it should not be offered by as many colleges and universities. In short, journalism, for all practical purposes, should not be offered by more than three or four tax-supported universities in any given state, depending on the state's population and number of media companies. This author suspects that some academicians would argue for no more than one or two state-supported institutions. Of course, private colleges and universities may offer whatever subjects their endowments can support. Journalism should not be offered in junior and community colleges. These colleges should offer general education courses so students who matriculate to four-year colleges and universities do not have to enroll in general education courses when they are juniors or seniors.

In the February 1981 issue of *Presstime*, Daniel E. Thornburgh, then chairman of the Department of Journalism at Eastern Illinois University, made the following assertions:

1. The jargon of communication theory and research affronts professional journalists.
2. Mass communication research has become too dominant in undergraduate journalism education.
3. With additional work in technical courses, in theory, and in mass communications research, academic work in the arts and sciences and in some . . . skills courses has suffered.
4. Life is now so complex that the journalism graduate from a four-year program may survive at an entry-level job, but is not prepared for career advancement. A fifth year of study for a professional degree in journalism is a possible answer.
5. Something needs to be done; professional journalism organizations should take a definite and unified stand as to the type of journalism program that should be recognized for accreditation purposes.[62]

Thornburgh's first three assertions have been mentioned elsewhere and commented on, but the last two have not. A few schools of journalism offered programs that began at the fifth year. For example, Columbia University's so-called professional program was actually a fifth-year program that allowed a student to earn the master's degree. The University of California at Berkeley had a similar program. Today, many schools of journalism have one or more master's degree programs. Some of these have been designed for students who wish to advance in their chosen career. In essence, these programs offer what Thornburgh mentioned in number four. Whether professional journalism organizations could make a unified stand as to what type of journalism program should be offered is debatable, considering there are so many journalism organizations and associations in existence.

In 1982 Howard Fibich, then news editor of the *Milwaukee Journal*, spoke at the annual meeting of the Association for Education in Journalism and Mass Communications. Fibich mentioned the following:

> What newspapers need from journalism educators is not scholars versed in the mumbo-jumbo of research methodology. We need reporters and editors with solid liberal arts backgrounds who know how to interview, how to gather information from often reluctant sources, who can write intelligently and who can deal with the maze of statutes and decisions on libel, privacy, open records and open meetings.[63]

Without question, schools of journalism have strived for the above. Indeed, in the well-known accredited programs one will find faculty members who worked in journalism for a number of years. These faculty members provide a valuable service to the programs and the students.

In the November/December 1984 issue of the *ASNE Bulletin*, Rhea T. Eskew claimed that schools of journalism needed to hire professionals who love and believe strongly in journalism, especially newspaper journalism. Eskew wrote, "Someone who knows that accuracy in reporting and writing is the linchpin to public acceptance of newspapers. Someone with enthusiasm, a sense of excitement with current events and both an understanding and love of the language."[64]

Eskew, like Schwed, believed that journalism programs needed more faculty members who had professional media experience. Of course, as has been pointed out, whether most journalism programs can afford such individuals with numerous years of professional media experience is debatable. However, such hiring practices would be possible if professional organizations or corporations could be persuaded to support endowments that exist in the schools or programs or provide funding for new endowments for such positions.

In 1990 Orlando L. Taylor, in "The Education of Journalists and Mass Communications for the 21st Century: A Cultural Perspective," identified several contributions that educators could make in assisting journalists and mass communicators to perform their craft and to provide leadership more effectively. One of these contributions included changes in the curriculum. He claimed that educators needed to include courses that focused on "cultural and ethnographic topics." Of course, Taylor realized that few courses in journalism and mass communication actually incorporated such diverse topics.[65]

In 1994, in "Ph.D.s vs. Professional Skills," John Wicklein claimed that many programs in journalism will hire people with doctorates before they will hire people with professional experience but no doctorates. The reasons for this practice, according to Wicklein, are academic and economic. He wrote,

> First is the desire of administrators, envying the prestige of Ivy League schools, to turn their universities into great research institutions. Second is the demand in recent years for heavy budget cuts. Since administrators don't think journalists contribute "real" research, they use budget cuts as an excuse to ax the schools. Practical programs with small classes and computer labs cost a lot; conventional academic programs do not.[66]

The above points are certainly true. More and more colleges and universities are requiring faculty to have doctorates and to contribute scholarly articles to scholarly journals. This practice will not, in all likelihood, change. It is conceivable that administrators would become flexible if professional organizations or corporations provided funds for endowments for faculty members who had professional journalism experience but no doctorate. Regarding budget cuts, several journalism programs have been gutted during the past few years. Indeed, the University of Michigan and Oregon State University have lost or modified their journalism programs. Iowa State University's program was saved when certain news organizations came to its defense. Other programs, including those at Ohio State University, San Diego State University, and the University of Southern California, although not entirely cut, were merged with other areas of communication. This trend has occurred at other colleges and universities, too, primarily because college and university administrators do not know the differences between journalism and other areas of communication and because they know that merging two or more areas or departments may save the institution money. Today, college and university administrators have to cut costs, especially if they work at public-supported institutions. However, this is long overdue. Many public-supported institutions of higher education—like other public-supported entities—waste money. For example, generally administrators earn higher salaries than faculty members. Yet, few administrators teach one course, let alone three or four. There is an understood saying in education: the farther away one gets from the students, the more money she or he is inclined to earn. The question is, do institutions of higher education need as many administrators as most have? The answer is no. Many presidents at institutions of higher learning have built bureaucracies—that is, offices for this, offices for that—particularly during the past two decades. Most, if not all, of these offices are managed by vice presidents who earn considerably more than most faculty members. Some would argue that these vice presidents earn considerably more than all faculty members. Although one or two of these new offices may be important or crucial to the everyday operation of an institution, most of these new offices could be closed. Some would argue that these offices should be closed. When one considers how much money goes to these new offices (remember, these offices typically are headed by vice presidents and have more than one employee), the question has to be asked: are these offices providing enough service to the institution to offset the costs? Or can the duties of these newer offices be performed by personnel in older offices? Sometimes presidents establish layers for no reason other than to insulate themselves from the others on campuses, or so it seems to this author.

In 1994 Jerry Ceppos, then managing editor of the *San Jose Mercury News*, claimed that journalism majors were being prepared for the information superhighway. He stated,

> If I were an educator, I wouldn't worry about means of delivery; we can't predict what it's going to be, and it doesn't matter. I would teach students how to gather the information, how to analyze it and how to present it in an understandable way. Those skills will be important regardless of the methods of transmission.[67]

With the rapid changes in communications and in the dissemination of information, many faculty members in journalism programs believe that teaching students how to use the Internet and social media is important. However, most students will learn how to use these as well as others before they graduate from high school. Some students have been exposed to both before they entered high school. Thus, courses in journalism programs should not necessarily emphasize these tools as much as the basic skills: spelling, writing, editing, and so forth.

In 2002 Jack Shafer, then editor at large for *Slate*, interviewed four successful journalists. At least three had graduate degrees in journalism from prestigious universities. Although Shafer did not believe that people who desired to be journalists needed degrees in journalism, he suggested the following:

1. The required curriculum for a major in journalism should be one year.
2. The journalism program should have a journalistic canon that every journalism student must read.

3. The journalism program should require journalism students to use a typewriter, not a computer, to type several classic examples of journalism. Students should learn what the rhythms of great journalism are as a result.
4. Advertising and public relations programs should not be in journalism programs or departments.
5. Journalism majors should understand mathematics, including statistics and polling methodology.
6. Journalism majors should understand ethics, philosophy, and history and how each relates to journalism.[68]

Shafer's first suggestion may be difficult to implement, considering that faculty argue over which courses should become the core (required courses) and which courses should become electives. Faculty members also argue over how many hours should be required for a major. Of course, if the journalism program is accredited, faculty members generally have no choice regarding how many hours can be required. Some faculty members believe that accreditation prohibits students from enrolling in courses that will benefit them because the courses are not required and the students may select other electives. Whether accreditation is a plus or a minus for a journalism program depends on the mission and goals of the program. Few students know whether a program has been accredited. And these few may not care. However, administrators care. It is another notch in their illustrious career belt, even if they are not directly involved in the gathering of data or writing the final document—the self-study—for the accrediting body. At many programs, for instance, faculty members and even staff personnel are involved in doing the document. (This author has worked on several accreditation and re-accreditation documents, which was a learning experience, to say the least.)

Shafer's second suggestion should be seriously considered by journalism faculty members. There are numerous articles and books that undergraduates and graduates in journalism should be required to read and analyze.

His third suggestion could be assigned, but more than likely students would use computers, not typewriters. Shafer feared that if computers were used, students would merely download the articles, which would negate the purpose of the exercise.

His fourth suggestion is sound. If advertising and public relations exist in a department or school of journalism, then both should be removed. In fact, in this author's opinion, advertising and public relations should be moved to the department that has marketing because both are more suited, philosophically speaking, to marketing than journalism. Or both could form a new department. This action—more than likely—would end numerous arguments and disputes among faculty members who find themselves in a department or school of journalism that has advertising and public relations.

Shafer's fifth suggestion is also sound. Students majoring in journalism need to understand mathematics, statistics, and how to conduct a poll or survey. Or they should know how to interpret the results of a poll or survey for an audience.

His sixth suggestion is valid. Students emphasizing journalism need to understand journalism ethics. They need to understand how philosophy relates to their chosen major. They need to understand the history of journalism.

In 2009 Richard Sine posted an article on the *Huffington Post* in which he reacted to the growth in enrollment in graduate schools of journalism. Sine could not believe that so many students were pursuing graduate degrees in a discipline for which there were few jobs. In fact, he advised deans of graduate schools of journalism to close the doors. Or at least decrease enrollments. Sine worked for various newspapers before he became a freelance writer. He studied business journalism on a fellowship and learned that students in business schools were much better prepared for employment than the students in journalism.[69]

Whether graduate schools of journalism should be closed is debatable, considering that many graduate schools of journalism offer more areas of study in addition to journalism. However, considering what has happened to the media, enrollments in schools of journalism should be lower. Far too many students who have similar problems as undergraduates have been admitted to graduate programs. In short, many graduate students do not write well and many do not know how to do research or how to write a research paper.

In 2009 Malcolm Gladwell, a popular writer for the *New Yorker* who has written a few best-selling books, told a reporter at *Time* that he would tell young aspiring journalists not to attend journalism schools. He claimed they should study another subject then write about it.[70]

This author agrees to a certain extent with Gladwell. If a young aspiring student desires to work in journalism, she should major or at least minor in a subject other than journalism. Of course, many colleges and universities allow students to major and minor in more than one subject. If this is the case, the student could get a major in accounting, biology, economics, finance, marketing, political science, or statistics, to mention a few, and another major or minor in journalism.

STUDIES ABOUT JOURNALISM EDUCATION
Edwin O. Haroldsen and Kenneth E. Harvey of Brigham Young University surveyed 313 magazine editors in 1979 and learned the following:

1. Editors of magazines questioned the quality of journalism education based on their experience with students who majored in journalism.
2. Students who majored in journalism did not have an understanding of the English language.
3. Students who majored in journalism were not proficient in copyediting.[71]

At the time of the survey, there were not many schools of journalism that specialized in magazine journalism. However, those that did were not doing well. Indeed, the survey revealed that these programs needed to change the curriculum or emphasis.

In 1980 Gordon Mills, Kenneth Harvey, and Leland Warnick of Brigham Young University surveyed 366 daily and 300 weekly newspapers in the country. Eighty (27 percent) of the weekly newspaper surveys and 147 (40 percent) of the daily newspaper surveys were returned. The responses indicated the following:

1. Weekly newspapers provided significant employment opportunities for journalism graduates, yet many weekly editors and publishers believed students were trained more for large, daily newspapers.
2. The news executives were disgusted at the lack of knowledge of basic grammar, punctuation, and spelling demonstrated by many journalism graduates.
3. Some news executives were hiring people who had majored in something other than journalism to fill their editorial positions.
4. Very few publications hesitated to hire recent journalism graduates as long as they were qualified.[72]

The first result from the survey should be considered by every educator who teaches courses in journalism. For too many years the weekly has been overlooked by most schools of journalism. Only a few schools have included in their course offerings one or two courses that deal specifically with the weekly. Perhaps a solution to this problem would be the implementation of either an organization or association on a college or university campus by the weeklies that serve the college's community. After all, there are numerous state colleges and universities trying to compete with one another on a large scale. Usually the large, greatly funded institution wins. Such colleges and universities offer, in addition to the typical bachelor's degree, the master's degree and, in some instances, the doctorate. Seldom can the smaller colleges and universities compare in quality. Thus, it would be to the smaller institutions' advantage if such an organization existed. Not only would the weeklies benefit, but the colleges and universities would have access to professionals and possible positions for graduates. In addition, the schools of journalism undoubtedly would increase their course offerings dealing with weeklies.

The third point must be considered. Certain newspapers are hiring graduates that majored in something other than journalism. If this becomes a huge problem, the smaller schools of journalism may find themselves in trouble. The larger, ACEJMC-accredited programs will survive, however, because of their reputations.

In January 1984, the School of Journalism at the University of Oregon published a study entitled *Planning for Curricular Change in Journalism Education.* The study was concerned with the future of journalism and mass communication education at colleges and universities in the United States. Surveys were sent to different groups, including top executives of all professional and industry organizations represented in the Council of Affiliates of the Association for Education in Journalism and Mass Communication. This group included newspaper publishers, editors, advertising agency executives, public relations executives, and broadcasting executives, among others. The results of this survey included the following:

1. Use professionals for special seminars.
2. Students need to learn media management.
3. Reduce the number of journalism courses; increase the number of liberal arts courses.
4. Reduce the number of journalism courses; increase the number of basic skills courses.
5. Implement stricter standards so weak students are weeded out.
6. Students need a better understanding of the industry.
7. Students need a more realistic setting, not just a typical classroom.
8. Students need to learn to think creatively.
9. Students need more mid-career training.
10. Students need to spend less time in the classroom and more time doing field work.[73]

The results were similar to comments made by other professionals. However, there were fresh comments, too. For example, the first comment. If programs offer special seminars, then faculty should be encouraged to bring in professionals. Professionals tend to provide insight that faculty members lack. Regarding the fourth comment, many faculty members and administrators believe there are enough skills courses in the curriculum. However, this comment should be considered. The fifth comment should be considered by all faculty and administrators. Students who do not know how to write should not be admitted to journalism programs. Regarding the sixth comment, faculty members may consider taking their classes on field trips to different media companies. The eighth comment has been considered by many programs. New courses that require creative thought have been added to the curriculum.

The results of the study persuaded faculty members at the University of Oregon to change the program in the School of Journalism. Because the study encompassed opinions and recommendations from practicing professionals and educators throughout the country, it was applicable to most programs in the country. Although certain recommendations, such as emphasizing the liberal arts, theory, and research, were adhered to by prominent programs, professional organizations for media personnel reacted somewhat negatively to the changes that occurred. For instance, in "When Northwest Editors Got Fed Up with Local J-Schools, They Started Their Own Rating System," Jack R. Hart pointed out that newspaper publishers and editors in the northwest severely criticized specific journalism programs primarily because of the de-emphasis on print journalism. Hart mentioned, however, that few professionals had any sense of the pressures journalism faculty faced regarding the direct relationship between tenure and conducting research. He also mentioned that few professionals were aware of the extremely low salaries of journalism faculty as well as the extremely low salaries offered by newspapers, which, of course, was one of the reasons for fewer students desiring to major in journalism.[74]

The professionals, through the organization Allied Daily Newspapers (now Pacific Northwest Newspaper Association), an industry group, founded the Journalism Education Committee, which initiated a university visitation program to evaluate schools and departments of journalism. Teams of three to five professionals visited eleven campuses in 1988. Specific programs were criticized for certain problems. However, the group provided funding to ten of the eleven programs primarily to help the programs correct the problems cited by the team.

In 1988 the committee met, evaluated the first round of visits, and recommended continuing the program.[75]

Such an endeavor by a group of professionals is commendable. Whether such activity should be performed by other professional organizations or associations that represent a geographic region is anyone's guess. However, having professionals serve on a panel or board created by each department or school of journalism would be beneficial, even if journalism faculty members did not wish to have their journalism program evaluated by a committee made up entirely of publishers, editors, and broadcasters.

In 1989, in *Challenges and Opportunities in Journalism and Mass Communication Education: A Report of the Task Force on the Future of Journalism and Mass Communication Education*, the Task Force described the characteristics of a well-prepared student who has majored in journalism:

> A well-prepared graduate will possess (1) a set of field-related skills; (2) a broad education grounded in the liberal arts; (3) a value-system that emphasizes public service; and (4) the ability to integrate these things "in relation to the life and work of the world."[76]

The Task Force emphasized liberal education:

> We want our students to have a liberal education not just to furnish them with facts and concepts that will give them something to communicate about as communication practitioners. We want them to be thinking, analytical, problem-solving human beings with ethical standards and an open-mindedness that will serve them well whether they are in pursuit of a story or in pursuit of a philosophy of life.[77]

If administrators and faculty members did not change their programs in journalism after reading the University of Oregon's study, they most certainly did after reading this report. Changes were made, especially to the curriculum.

In 1993 at the Association for Education in Journalism and Mass Communication conference in Kansas City, specifically, in the session "Revamping Journalism Education," panelists recommended the following:

1. Journalism programs need to hire experts in various fields, not just in journalism.
2. The curriculum in journalism needs to include a variety of information to give students "a better sense of reality."
3. Journalism programs should persuade newspaper companies to give "state-of-the-art equipment."

4. Journalism programs should develop stronger ties with high school journalism teachers and advisers so would-be journalism majors are better prepared.
5. Journalism programs need to put more emphasis on critical thinking as well as pay more attention to human values and less to technology.
6. Courses in basic ethics need to be added to the journalism curriculum.[78]

A few prominent programs have hired people from various fields, not just journalism. The second, fifth, and sixth suggestions have been considered by most, if not all, journalism programs. Although newspaper companies should provide equipment, particularly to the journalism programs that do not receive adequate funding, many have other problems to consider. The fourth suggestion has been considered by many journalism programs. However, this author believes that only a few have been successful in developing strong ties with various high school journalism teachers and advisers.

On behalf of the Carnegie Corporation of New York and the Carnegie-Knight Initiative on the Future of Journalism Education, McKinsey and Company in 2005 conducted one-to-one interviews with forty prominent leaders of the journalism industry. Persons interviewed identified the following needs:

1. A need for analytical thinkers with a strong ethical sense, as well as journalism skills;
2. A need for specialized expertise: insights into medicine, economics, and other complex topics, and firsthand knowledge of societies, languages, religions, and cultures; and
3. A need for the best writers, the most curious reporters.[79]

The results were taken seriously by the Carnegie-Knight Initiative on the Future of Journalism Education. Supported by two foundations (Carnegie and Knight), the organization has provided millions of dollars to journalism programs that have developed initiatives in response to one or more of the above observations.

BRIEF COMMENTS ABOUT ACCREDITATION AND THE ACCREDITING COUNCIL ON EDUCATION IN JOURNALISM AND MASS COMMUNICATIONS

Before administrators and faculty members of a journalism program consider accreditation and what it involves, the person in charge of the program should obtain a copy of the booklet *Journalism and Mass Communication Accredita-*

tion from the Accrediting Council on Education in Journalism and Mass Communications (ACEJMC). This booklet provides information about the ACEJMC and accreditation, such as the council's mission statement, its vision statement, the purposes and benefits of accreditation, the history and structure of the council, the principles of accreditation, the policies of accreditation, the mechanisms of accreditation, the accrediting standards, the accredited programs, the member organizations, the accrediting committee members, and the accrediting council members. Perhaps the most important information is in the mechanisms of accreditation and the accrediting standards. These sections discuss the accrediting process, the self-study document, the fees, and the nine standards, among other information.

Although the council's booklet discusses the significance of accreditation, one should remember that accreditation is self-serving—that is, it is only important to the administrators and faculty members of the program and institution, not necessarily the public at large or the students. There are numerous non-accredited programs that provide students with a good education. In some instances, some of these non-accredited programs provide students with a better educational experience than what is offered at numerous accredited programs. Therefore, accreditation does not necessarily mean that a program is one of the best in the country. Accreditation merely means that a program has evaluated itself based on nine standards, then asked a team of three, four, five, or six members to spend a few days on campus to evaluate the program. This author finds more than one problem with accreditation. For instance, a program's self-study will more than likely be biased and exaggerated. After all, is it in administrators' best interest to report every fact, including problems, about a program? The answer is no. Furthermore, the members of the team have such a brief period of time to evaluate the program that they will more than likely miss several problems that were not discussed in the self-study. The team's visit should last at least five days. In addition, another question that needs to be asked is, who are the members of the team? Are these individuals qualified? What are their educational backgrounds? What are their professional backgrounds? Do they know what to look for when they visit a program? Do they know which professors will have information that was not in the self-study? Members of a typical team may include one or two administrators from a college of journalism or mass communications; one or two faculty members from a college of journalism or mass communications, a school of journalism or mass communications, or a department of journalism or mass communications; and possibly a professional who works or worked for a media company. In short, this author finds major weaknesses in the accreditation process.

As mentioned, the program has to pay a fee as well as all expenses associated with its evaluation. If accredited, the program has to pay annual dues. Considering the time and effort faculty members and administrators have to put into the self-study report, not to mention the thousands of dollars in expenses, accreditation should be seriously discussed by everyone involved before it is undertaken. Furthermore, if accredited, a program must do another self-study for re-accreditation in just a few years. Consequently, accreditation must be worth the effort, time, and expense. Otherwise, it should not be undertaken.

The author suggests that before a program begins the accreditation process it should list the strengths and weaknesses for accreditation. It may even wish to list the opportunities as well as the threats accreditation may provide. In short, a SWOT (Strengths Weaknesses Opportunities Threats) analysis or something similar should be performed. Faculty members and administrators must remember that accreditation forces the program to have a specific number of courses or hours for the major. Faculty members and administrators must remember, too, that accreditation requires an emphasis in liberal arts courses. The question that must be asked is: does accreditation restrict the student's education? Are liberal arts courses more important than, say, numerous courses in accounting, finance, marketing, management, or some other subject that is not considered a liberal art? This is another problem this author has with accreditation. For instance, if an institution has an accredited program in journalism, and the institution requires 120 hours for a bachelor's degree, for a student majoring in journalism at least 65 hours has to be in liberal arts and sciences. This leaves 30 to possibly 39 hours for the major in journalism and a few hours for a minor, unless the minor is one of the liberal arts or sciences. Does this leave enough hours for the student to emphasize another discipline that will help him or her have an advantage over someone else? This is the question faculty members and administrators should ask.

RECOMMENDATIONS

As this chapter has shown, there are problems with journalism education. As enrollment figures have increased over the years, members of the media as well as journalism educators have discussed several problems. And they are asking for something to be done. If directors of journalism programs do not heed the warnings by professionals, they may find their graduates selling coffee, burgers, or clothes. They certainly will not find their graduates working at newspapers, radio stations, television stations, or other media. As pointed out by Ken Harvey and Ronald Smith, "Journalism educators and journalism professionals are at such odds over how prospective journalists should be trained that an educational revolution could be imminent."[80] Besides, professionals who work in the media realize that a sizable number of print journalists who have received Pulitzer Prizes never studied journalism and that a sizable number of broadcast journalists who have received Alfred I. Du Pont Awards never studied journalism.[81] In short, one does not need to study journalism or broadcasting to become a successful journalist.

In addition to the recommendations and suggestions that have been mentioned, the following should be considered by administrators and faculty members in journalism programs:

1. All journalism programs should require students to pass entrance examinations before they are admitted to study journalism. In fact, the ACEJMC should include this as one of its standards for accreditation.
2. All journalism programs should require students to have a high grade point average before they are admitted to study journalism. (This author believes that students should have a 3.0 on a 4.0 scale based on at least forty-five hours of academic credit.)
3. Knowledge of basic writing skills, including grammar, punctuation, editing, and spelling, should be required of every major.
4. There should be more journalism courses available to students. These courses should be diverse in content—that is, cover such topics as the new technology, marketing, ethics, journalism for weeklies, and global journalism, to mention a few.
5. Internships in which students receive academic credit should be available to all majors. However, internships should be reserved for those students who have achieved a high grade point average based on at least twenty-four hours of academic credit in journalism. (This author believes that internship advisors should realize that a student's performance as an intern reflects on the program. Consequently, internships should be reserved for those students who have excelled in the classroom.)
6. Skill-course faculty members should have professional experience. How many years of experience should be determined by journalism faculty. Of course, faculty members should consider where their department or school is located—that is, is it in a four-year college, university, or research university—for part of their decision. For instance, the journalism faculty at a state-supported four-year college may not require as many years of professional experience as the journalism faculty at a state-supported research university. Of course, there may be some state-supported four-year

colleges that require more years of professional experience than many state-supported research universities.

7. Journalism faculty members who teach in predominately professional programs—that is, a program that prepares students for entry-level positions—may wish to consider de-emphasizing theory courses at the undergraduate level.

8. The doctorate should not necessarily be a requirement for faculty advancement unless the faculty member teaches primarily theory courses.

9. Students who major in journalism should be forced to enroll in courses such as accounting, business administration, business law, computer science, economics, finance, foreign language, history, information systems, marketing, mathematics, one or more natural sciences, philosophy, political science, and statistics, to mention a few.

10. Administrators and faculty in journalism programs should build strong relationships with professionals. In fact, prominent professionals should be asked to sit on boards that meet and provide guidance to the programs. Professionals should be invited to speak to students enrolled in particular courses. They should be invited to speak to members of organizations whenever the organizations meet.

11. Advertising and public relations, if these disciplines exist in a journalism program, should be separated from such programs. In fact, this author believes both disciplines should be moved to the department that has marketing. Or, if the disciplines are large enough (based on number of faculty, the curriculum, and the number of students) to warrant a department, then a new department, preferably in a college of business, should be developed.

FINAL COMMENT

Although this suggestion has been mentioned, government officials, including governors, their appointed administrators, and members of boards of regents should evaluate the number of journalism programs that exist at state-supported institutions in their states to determine whether every journalism program is needed. (In fact, this should be done for any academic program that does not offer required courses—such as English—that must be passed by every student and/or for any academic program that exists at several state-supported institutions.) In short, the question—does the state need as many of these academic programs as it has—needs to be asked. Higher education is an expensive proposition to the state government and to the students. Tuition and fees increase substantially every year. Just ask any student. Not all state-supported, four-year colleges or universities need the same academic programs. As mentioned, states do not need more than three or four academic programs in journalism, unless the states have a large population and numerous media companies. In fact, some states do not need more than one or two academic programs in journalism. Today, most programs in journalism are producing graduates who will never find employment in their chosen major. Are all of these expensive programs necessary? The answer is no.

NOTES

1. Betty Medsger, "The Evolution of Journalism Education in the United States," *Making Journalists: Diverse Models, Global Issues*, edited by Hugo de Burgh, Foreword by James Curran (London: Routledge, 2005), 206.

2. Joseph A. Mirando, "Training and Educating Journalists," *American Journalism: History, Principles, Practices*, edited by W. David Sloan and Lisa Mullikin Parcell (Jefferson, N.C.: McFarland and Company, Inc., Publishers, 2002), 76.

3. Mirando, "Training and Educating Journalists," 77.

4. De Forest O'Dell, *The History of Journalism Education in the United States* (New York: Teachers College, Columbia University, Bureau of Publications, 1935), 1.

5. O'Dell, *The History of Journalism Education in the United States*, 9.

6. O'Dell, *The History of Journalism Education in the United States*, 5.

7. O'Dell, *The History of Journalism Education in the United States*, 5–19; Joseph A. Mirando, "The First College Journalism Students: Answering Robert E. Lee's Offer of a Higher Education," ED 402 599 (Washington, D.C.: Educational Resources Information Center [ERIC], August 1995), 7–15.

8. Frederic Hudson, *Journalism in the United States* (New York: Harper and Brothers, 1873), 713.

9. James Melvin Lee, *Instruction in Journalism in Institutions of Higher Learning*, Bulletin No. 21 (U.S. Department of the Interior, Bureau of Education, 1918), 8.

10. *The University of Pennsylvania Catalogue, 1893–94* (Philadelphia: The University of Pennsylvania, 1893), 111; Vernon Nash, *Educating for Journalism*, Ed.D. Dissertation (New York: Teachers College, Columbia University, 1938), 14–15.

11. *University Daily Kansan*, May 18, 1934; O'Dell, *The History of Journalism Education in the United States*, 49.

12. William H. Taft, "Establishing the School of Journalism," *Missouri Historical Review*, 84 (October 1989), 63.

13. Joseph Pulitzer, "The College of Journalism," *North American Review*, 178 (May 1904), 641.

14. O'Dell, *The History of Journalism Education in the United States*, 84; Lee, *Instruction in Journalism in Institutions of Higher Learning*, Bulletin No. 21, 13.

15. Leon Whipple, "Journalism," *The Survey* 60 (June 1, 1928), 292; Paul L. Dressel, *Liberal Education and Journalism* (New York: Teachers College, Columbia University, Bureau of Publications, 1960), 24–25.

16. "Editorial," *Journalism Bulletin* 4 (1927), 25; Albert Alton Sutton, *Education for Journalism in the United States From Its Beginning to 1940* (Evanston, Ill.: Northwestern University Press, 1945), 16.

17. Sutton, *Education for Journalism in the United States From Its Beginning to 1940*, 16.

18. Lee, *Instruction in Journalism in Institutions of Higher Learning*, Bulletin No. 11, 16, 27; Sutton, *Education for Journalism in the United States From Its Beginning to 1940*, 17.

19. "Directory of Teachers of Journalism in Colleges and Universities in the United States," *Journalism Quarterly* 9 (1932), 104; "Directory of Teachers of Journalism in Colleges and Universities in the United States," *Journalism Quarterly* 11 (1934), 110.

20. Sutton, *Education for Journalism in the United States From Its Beginning to 1940*, 18–20.

21. Nash, *Educating for Journalism*, 23; Mirando, "Training and Education of Journalists," 81.

22. Mirando, "Training and Education of Journalists," 82; Sutton, *Education for Journalism in the United States From Its Beginning to 1940*, 52–53, 70–71, 84–85.

23. Sutton, *Education for Journalism in the United States From Its Beginning to 1940*, 71, 86, 104.

24. Norval Neil Luxon, "Education for Journalism," *Education for the Professions*, edited by Lloyd E. Bauch (Washington, D.C.: U.S. Government Printing Office, 1955), 106; Dressel, *Liberal Education and Journalism*, 36.

25. Everett M. Rogers, *A History of Communication Study: A Biographical Approach* (New York: The Free Press, 1994), 27–29.

26. Rogers, *A History of Communication Study*, 27–29.

27. Wm. David Sloan, "In Search of Itself: A History of Journalism Education," *Makers of the Media Mind: Journalism Educators and Their Ideas*, edited by Wm. David Sloan (Hillsdale, N.J.: Lawrence Erlbaum Associates, Publishers, 1990), 17.

28. Mirando, "Training and Education of Journalists," 84.

29. Mirando, "Training and Education of Journalists," 84.

30. Sloan, "In Search of Itself," 19.

31. Sutton, *Education for Journalism*, 26–35; Dressel, *Liberal Education and Journalism*, 34–35; Association for Education in Journalism and Mass Communications (www.aejmc.com/home/about/aejmc-history/) (28 October 2010).

32. American Association of Teachers of Journalism and American Association of Schools and Departments of Journalism, Council on Education, "Principles and Standards of Education for Journalism," *Journalism Bulletin* 1 (1924), 30–31; Sutton, *Education for Journalism*, 26–35; Dressel, *Liberal Education and Journalism*, 34–35; "History and Structure of ACEJMC," *Journalism and Mass Communications Accreditation 2009–2010* (Lawrence: ACEJMC, University of Kansas, 2009), 11–12.

33. Dressel, *Liberal Education and Journalism*, 21–22.

34. Charles F. Wingate, *Views and Interviews on Journalism* (New York: F. B. Patterson, 1875), 15–16.

35. Dressel, *Liberal Education and Journalism*, 24.

36. Dressel, *Liberal Education and Journalism*, 25.

37. Dressel, *Liberal Education and Journalism*, 25.

38. Dressel, *Liberal Education and Journalism*, 25.

39. Commission on Freedom of the Press, *A Free and Responsible Press* (Chicago: University of Chicago Press, 1974), 78.

40. John Tebbel, "What's Happening to Journalism Education?" *Saturday Review* (October 12, 1963), 52.

41. David Boroff, "What Ails the Journalism Schools?" *Harper's* (October 1965), 80, 82, 87.

42. Boroff, "What Ails the Journalism Schools?" 80, 82, 87.

43. M. L. Stein, "Journalism Education—A Matter of Co-Existence," *Saturday Review* (October 9, 1971), 71–73.

44. Lloyd W. Brown, Jr., "Editors Criticize J-Schools Curricula at Symposium," *Editor and Publisher* (June 24, 1972), 9.

45. Hillier Krieghbaum, "J-School Training Criticized in ANPA-AEJ 'Rap' Session," *Editor and Publisher* (November 10, 1973), 72.

46. Jim Scott, "Editors Give Journalism Education Failing Grade," *Editor and Publisher* (November 2, 1974), 10.

47. Ted Bush, "Now Is the Time for All Good Editors to Gripe About J-Schools," *ASNE Bulletin* (November/December 1974), 20–21.

48. Ronald Farrar, "J-Schools: A Nouveau Riche Environment?" *Nieman Reports* (Autumn/Winter 1975), 59–60.

49. Ben Bagdikian, "Woodstein U," *Atlantic* (March 1977), 83.

50. Bagdikian, "Woodstein U," 86–87.

51. Bagdikian, "Woodstein U," 86–87.

52. Mal Deans, "New Technology Results in Better-Trained J-Students," *Editor and Publisher* (August 25, 1977), 15.

53. Deans, "New Technology Results in Better-Trained J-Students," 15.

54. Darrell Berkheimer, "J-Schools Should Hire Reporters, Not Bookworms," *Editor and Publisher* (September 1, 1979), 5.

55. Berkheimer, "J-Schools Should Hire Reporters, Not Bookworms," 5.

56. Creed Black, "Journalism Education: A Publisher's View," *The Quill* (October 1979), 14.

57. Black, "Journalism Education: A Publisher's View," 14.

58. Warren Schwed, "What's Wrong with Journalism Education?" *Editor and Publisher* (November 15, 1980), 15.

59. Schwed, "What's Wrong with Journalism Education?" 15.

60. Schwed, "What's Wrong with Journalism Education?" 15.

61. Schwed, "What's Wrong with Journalism Education?" 15.

62. Daniel E. Thornburgh, "A Professor Worries About J-School Trends," *Presstime* (February 1981), 27.

63. Charles-Gene McDaniel, "How to Make Schools of Journalism Better," *Editor and Publisher* (August 7, 1982), 10.

64. Rhea T. Eskew, "Publisher's Lament: Too Many Under-Motivated, Shabbily Trained and Generally Ill-Equipped J-School Graduates," *ASNE Bulletin* (November/December 1984), 6.

65. Orlando L. Taylor, "The Education of Journalists and Mass Communications for the 21st Century: A Cultural Perspective," *INSIGHTS* (April 1990), 6–14, 43.

66. John Wicklein, "Ph.D.s vs. Professional Skills," *ASNE Bulletin* (November/December 1994), 20.

67. Tony Case, "A Need to Communicate," *Editor and Publisher* (October 15, 1994), 30.

68. Jack Shafer, "Can J-School Be Saved?: Professional Advice for Columbia University," *Slate* (October 7, 2002) (www.slate.com/toolbar .aspx?action=print&id=2071993) (19 September 2010).

69. Richard Sine, "Close the J-Schools," *Huffington Post* (July 15, 2009) (www .huffingtonpost.com/richard-sine/close-the-j-schools-b-232174.html) (24 July 2009).

70. "Malcolm Gladwell: Aspiring Journalists Should Skip J-School," *Huffington Post* (October 20, 2009) (www.huffingtonpost.com/2009/10/20/malcolm-gladwell-aspiring-n-327161.html) (25 October 2010).

71. Edwin O. Haroldsen and Kenneth E. Harvey, "Frowns Greet New J-Grads in Magazine Job Market," *Journalism Educator* (July 1979), 26.

72. Gordon Mills, Kenneth Harvey, and Leland Warnick, "Newspaper Editors Point to J-Grad Deficiencies," *Journalism Educator* (July 1980), 19.

73. *Planning for Curricular Change in Journalism Education: Project on the Future of Journalism and Mass Communication Education*, Second Edition (Eugene: School of Journalism, University of Oregon, November 1987), 30–31.

74. Jack R. Hart, "When Northwest Editors Got Fed Up with Local J-Schools, They Started Their Own Rating System," *ASNE Bulletin* (April 1990), 18–21.

75. Hart, "When Northwest Editors Got Fed Up with Local J-Schools, They Started Their Own Rating System," 21.

76. *Challenges and Opportunities in Journalism and Mass Communication Education: A Report of the Task Force on the Future of Journalism and Mass Communication Education*, Educator/Curriculum Report (Columbia, S.C.: Association for Education in Journalism and Mass Communication, 1989), A-4.

77. *Challenges and Opportunities in Journalism and Mass Communication Education*, A-8.

78. M. L. Stein, "Revamping Journalism Education," *Editor and Publisher* (August 28, 1993), 13.

79. Susan King, "The Carnegie-Knight Initiative on the Future of Journalism Education: Improving How Journalists Are Educated and How Their Audiences Are

Informed," *A Way Forward: Solving the Challenges of the News Frontier: A Report of Carnegie Corporation of New York* (New York: Carnegie Corporation of New York, 2010), 38.

80. Ken Harvey and Ronald Smith, "News Execs Urge Major Overhaul of Journalism Training Program," *Editor and Publisher* (March 6, 1982), 10.

81. Medsger, "The Evolution of Journalism Education in the United States," 222.

Selected Bibliography

A Way Forward: Solving the Challenges of the News Frontier: A Report of Carnegie Corporation of New York. (2010). New York: Carnegie Corporation of New York.

Allan, Stuart, ed. (2005). *Journalism: Critical Issues.* Berkshire, England: Open University Press, McGraw-Hill Education.

Atwan, Robert, Barry Orton, and William Vesterman, eds. (1978). *American Mass Media.* New York: Random House.

Bagdikian, Ben. (1972). *The Effete Conspiracy.* New York: Harper and Row.

———. (1992). *The Media Monopoly.* Boston: Beacon Press.

———. (2004). *The New Media Monopoly*, 7th ed. Boston: Beacon Press.

Beckett, Charles. (2008). *Super Media: Saving Journalism So It Can Save the World.* Malden, Mass.: Blackwell Publishing.

Belsey, Andrew, and Ruth Chadwick, eds. (1992). *Ethical Issues in Journalism and the Media.* New York: Routledge.

Bennett, W. Lance. (1983). *News: The Politics of Illusion.* New York: Longman.

Berry, Thomas. (1976). *Journalism in America.* New York: Hastings House.

Blauch, Lloyd E., ed. (1955). *Education for the Professions.* Washington, D.C.: U.S. Government Printing Office.

Bleyer, Willard, ed. (1918). *The Profession of Journalism.* Boston: Atlantic Monthly Press.

———. (1927). *Main Currents in the History of American Journalism.* Boston: Houghton Mifflin Co.

———. (1931). "What Schools of Journalism Are Trying to Do." *Journalism Quarterly* 8: 35–44.

Bronstein, Carolyn, and Stephen Vaughn. (June 1998). "Willard G. Bleyer and the Relevance of Journalism Education." *Journalism Monographs*, Vol. 166.

Bryant, Jennings, and Dolf Zillmann, eds. (1994). *Media Effects: Advances in Theory and Research.* Hillsdale, N.J.: Lawrence Erlbaum Associates.

Burrows, William. (1977). *On Reporting the News.* New York: New York University Press.

Butler, Nicholas Murray. (1910). *Education in the United States.* New York: American Book Co.

Camp, Eugene M. (1888). *Journalists: Born or Made?* Philadelphia: Philadelphia Social Science Association.

Canons of Journalism. (1922). American Society of Newspaper Editors.

Casebier, Allan, and Janet Casebier, eds. (1978). *Social Responsibilities of the Mass Media.* Washington, D.C.: University Press of America.

Casey, Ralph D. (March 1932). "Journalism, Technical Training and the Social Sciences." *Journalism Quarterly* 9: 31–45.

Challenges and Opportunities in Journalism and Mass Communication Education: A Report of the Task Force on the Future of Journalism and Mass Communication Education. (1989). Columbia, S.C.: Association for Education in Journalism and Mass Communications.

Charnley, Mitchell. (1963). *Reporting.* New York: Holt, Rinehart and Winston.

Christians, Clifford G., John P. Ferre, and P. Mark Fackler. (1993). *Good News: Social Ethics and the Press.* New York: Oxford University Press.

Cohen, Elliot D., ed. (1992). *Philosophical Issues in Journalism.* New York: Oxford University Press.

Commission on Freedom of the Press. (1974). *A Free and Responsible Press.* Chicago: University of Chicago Press.

Coppa, Frank J., ed. (1979). *Screen and Society.* Chicago: Nelson-Hall.

Cropp, Fritz, Cynthia M. Frisby, and Dean Mills, eds. (2003). *Journalism across Cultures.* Ames: Iowa State Press.

Curry, Richard O., ed. (1988). *Freedom at Risk: Secrecy, Censorship, and Repression in the 1980s.* Philadelphia: Temple University Press.

Dahlgren, Peter, and Colin Sparks, eds. (1992). *Journalism and Popular Culture.* Newbury Park, Calif.: SAGE Publications.

Davis, Richard. (1992). *The Press and American Politics: The New Mediator.* White Plains, N.Y.: Longman Publishing Group.

de Burgh, Hugo, ed. (2005). *Making Journalists: Diverse Models, Global Issues.* Foreword by James Curran. London: Routledge.

Demac, Donna A. (1988). *Liberty Denied: The Current Rise of Censorship in America.* New York: PEN American Center.

Dickson, Tom. (2000). *Mass Media Education in Transition.* Mahwah, N.J.: Lawrence Erlbaum Associates.

Dizard, Wilson, Jr. (1994). *Old Media New Media: Mass Communications in the Information Age.* New York: Longman Publishing Group.

Downing, John, and Charles Husband. (2005). *Representing "Race": Racisms, Ethnicities and Media.* London: SAGE Publications.

Downs, Robert B., and Ralph E. McCoy, eds. (1984). *The First Freedom Today: Critical Issues Relating to Censorship and to Intellectual Freedom.* Chicago: American Library Association.

Dressel, Paul L. (1960). *Liberal Education and Journalism*. New York: Bureau of Publications, Teachers College, Columbia University.

Elliott, Deni, ed. (1986). *Responsible Journalism*. Beverly Hills, Calif.: SAGE Publications.

Emery, Edwin, and Joseph P. McKerns. (1987). "AEJMC: 75 Years in the Making: A History of Organizing for Journalism and Mass Communication Education in the United States." *Journalism Monographs*, Vol. 104.

Emery, Michael, and Ted Curtis Smythe, eds. (1977). *Readings in Mass Communication*. Dubuque, Iowa: Wm. C. Brown Co.

Entman, Robert M., and Andrew Rojecki. (2000). *The Black Image in the White Mind: Media and Race in America*. Chicago: The University of Chicago Press.

Epstein, Edward Jay. (1975). *Between Fact and Fiction: The Problems of Journalism*. New York: Vintage Books.

Flexner, Abraham. (1930). *Universities: American, English, German*. New York: Oxford University Press.

Ford, James L. C. (1947). *A Study of the Pre-War Curricula of Selected Schools of Journalism*. Ph.D. Dissertation. Minneapolis: University of Minnesota.

Freeman, Douglas S. (1935). *R. E. Lee*. Vols. I, II, III, IV. New York: Charles Scribners' Sons.

Goldstein, Tom, ed. (1989). *Killing the Messenger: 100 Years of Media Criticism*. New York: Columbia University Press.

Graber, Doris A. (1993). *Mass Media and American Politics*. Washington, D.C.: Congressional Quarterly.

Hallin, Daniel C. (1994). *We Keep America on Top of the World: Television Journalism and the Public Sphere*. New York: Routledge.

Harrison, Jackie. (2006). *News*. New York: Routledge.

Harriss, Julian, Kelly Leiter, and Stanley Johnson. (1977). *The Complete Reporter*. New York: Macmillan.

Hausman, Carl. (1992). *Crisis of Conscience: Perspectives on Journalism Ethics*. New York: HarperCollins.

Hiebert, Ray, Donald Ungurait, and Thomas Bohn. (1979). *Mass Media II*. New York: Longman.

Hudson, Frederic. (1873). *Journalism in the United States*. New York: Harper and Brothers.

Hulteng, John L. (1979). *The News Media—What Makes Them Tick?* Englewood Cliffs, N.J.: Prentice-Hall.

Hulteng, John L., and Roy Paul Nelson. (1971). *The Fourth Estate*. New York: Harper and Row.

Hutchins, Robert M. (1936). *The Higher Learning in America*. New Haven, Conn.: Yale University Press.

Hyde, Grant M. (March 1937). "The Next Steps in Schools of Journalism." *Journalism Quarterly* 14: 35–41.

James, Henry. (1930). *Charles W. Eliot*. Vols. I, II. Boston: Houghton Mifflin Co.

Kaniss, Phyllis. (1991). *Making Local News.* Chicago: University of Chicago Press.

Kitty, Alexandra. (2005). *Don't Believe It! How Lies Become News.* New York: The Disinformation Company Ltd.

Koch, Tom. (1990). *The News as Myth: Fact and Context in Journalism.* Westport, Conn.: Greenwood Press.

Kohn, Bob. (2003). *Journalistic Fraud: How the* New York Times *Distorts the News and Why It Can No Longer Be Trusted.* Nashville, Tenn.: WND Books.

Krieghbaum, Hillier. (1972). *Pressures on the Press.* New York: Thomas Y. Crowell Co.

Lee, A., and Norman Soloman. (1990). *Unreliable Sources: A Guide to Detecting Bias in News Media.* New York: Carol Publishing Group.

Lee, Captain Robert E. (1924). *Recollections and Letters of General Robert E. Lee.* New York: Doubleday, Doran and Co.

Lee, James Melvin. (1918). *Instruction in Journalism in Institutions of Higher Education.* Bulletin No. 21. U.S. Department of the Interior, Bureau of Education.

Lichtenberg, Judith, ed. (1990). *Democracy and the Mass Media.* Cambridge, England: Cambridge University Press.

Macdonald, Myra. (2003). *Exploring Media Discourse.* London: Hodder Education Group: A Hodder Arnold Publication.

MacDougall, Curtis D. (1982). *Interpretative Reporting,* 8th ed. New York: Macmillan.

Mazzocco, Dennis W. (1994). *Networks of Power: Corporate TV's Threat to Democracy.* Boston: South End Press.

McCombs, Maxwell, Edna Einsiedel, and David Weaver. (1991). *Contemporary Public Opinion: Issues and the News.* Hillsdale, N.J.: Lawrence Erlbaum Associates.

McManus, John H. (1994). *Market-Driven Journalism: Let the Citizen Beware.* Thousand Oaks, Calif.: SAGE Publications.

McQuail, Denis. (2005). *McQuail's Mass Communication Theory,* 5th ed. London: SAGE Publications Ltd.

Medsger, Betty. (1996). *Winds of Change: Challenges Confronting Journalism Education.* Arlington, Va.: The Freedom Forum.

Minor, Dale. (1970). *The Information War.* New York: Hawthorn Books.

Miraldi, Robert. (1990). *Muckraking and Objectivity: Journalism's Colliding Traditions.* Westport, Conn.: Greenwood Press.

Mirando, Joseph A. (August 1995). "The First College Journalism Students: Answering Robert E. Lee's Offer of a Higher Education." ED 402 599. Washington, D.C.: Educational Resources Information Center (ERIC).

Nash, Vernon. (1938). *Education for Journalism.* New York: Bureau of Publications, Teachers College, Columbia University.

Nielsen Media Research 1992–1993 Report on Television. (1993). New York: Nielsen Media Research.

O'Dell, De Forest. (1935). *The History of Journalism Education in the United States.* New York: Bureau of Publications, Teachers College, Columbia University.

Olasky, Marvin. (1988). *Prodigal Press: The Anti-Christian Bias of the American News Media.* Westchester, Ill.: Crossway Books.

Pell, Eve. (1984). *The Big Chill*. Boston: Beacon Press.

Pippert, Wesley G. (1989). *An Ethics of News: A Reporter's Search for Truth*. Washington, D.C.: Georgetown University Press.

Planning for Curricular Change in Journalism Education: Project on the Future of Journalism and Mass Communication Education, 2nd edition. (November 1987). Eugene: School of Journalism, University of Oregon.

Pulitzer, Joseph. (May 1904). "The College of Journalism." *North American Review* 178: 641–80.

Rivers, William L. (1975). *The Mass Media: Reporting, Writing, Editing*. New York: Harper and Row.

Rivers, William L., Wilbur Schramm, and Clifford G. Christians. (1980). *Responsibility in Mass Communication*. New York: Harper and Row.

Rogers, Everette M. (1994). *A History of Communication Study: A Biographical Approach*. New York: The Free Press.

Rogers, Everette M., and Steven H. Chaffee. (December 1994). "Communication and Journalism from 'Daddy' Bleyer to Wilbur Schramm: A Palimpsest." *Journalism Monographs*, Vol. 148.

Rubin, Bernard, ed. (1980). *Small Voices and Great Trumpets*. New York: Praeger Publishers.

Rucker, Frank W. (1964). *Walter Williams*. Columbia: University of Missouri Press.

Ryan, Michael, and James Tankard, Jr. (1977). *Basic News Reporting*. Palo Alto, Calif.: Mayfield Publishing Co.

Schudson, Michael. (1978). *Discovering the News*. New York: Basic Books.

———. (2003). *The Sociology of News*. New York: W. W. Norton & Company.

Seitz, Don. (1924). *Joseph Pulitzer, His Life and Letters*. New York: Simon and Schuster.

Siebert, Fred S., Theodore Peterson, and Wilbur Schramm. (1973). *Four Theories of the Press*. Freeport, N.Y.: Books for Libraries Press.

Sloan, Wm. David, ed. (1990). *Makers of the Media Mind: Journalism Educators and Their Ideas*. Hillsdale, N.J.: Lawrence Erlbaum Associates.

Sloan, Wm. David, and Jean Burleson Mackay, eds. (2002). *Media Bias: Finding It, Fixing It*. Jefferson, N.C.: McFarland and Company.

Sloan, W. David, and Lisa Mullikin Parcell, eds. (2002). *American Journalism: History, Principles, Practices*. Jefferson, N.C.: McFarland and Company.

Stanley, Robert H., and Charles S. Steinberg. (1976). *The Media Environment*. New York: Hastings House.

Statement of Principles. (1975). American Society of News Editors.

Steadman, Jana. (Summer 2005). "TV Audience Special Study: African-American Audience." Nielsen Media Research.

Sutton, Albert Alton. (1945). *Education for Journalism in the United States from Its Beginning to 1940*. Evanston, Ill.: Northwestern University Press.

The Training of Journalists: A World-Wide Survey on the Training of Personnel for the Mass Media. (1958). Paris: UNESCO.

University of Missouri Bulletin. (October 15, 1959). Columbia: University of Missouri.

Ward, Stephen J. A. (2004). *The Invention of Journalism Ethics: The Path to Objectivity and Beyond.* Montreal: McGill-Queen's University Press.

Ward, Walter J., and Associates. (1973). *The Nature of News in Three Dimensions.* Stillwater: Oklahoma State University, Bureau of Media Research, School of Journalism and Broadcasting.

White, Andrew Dickson. (1914). *Autobiography.* Vol. I. New York: The Century Co.

White, H. A. (1907). *Robert E. Lee and the Southern Confederacy.* New York: G. P. Putnam's Sons.

Wicker, Tom. (1979). *On Press.* New York: Berkley Publishing.

Will, Allen Sinclair. (1931). *Education for Newspaper Life.* Newark, N.J.: The Essex Press.

Williams, Sara Lockwood. (1929). *Twenty Years of Education for Journalism: A History of the School of Journalism of the University of Missouri, Columbia, Missouri, U.S.A.* Columbia, Mo.: E. W. Stephens Publishing Co.

Willis, Jim. (1990). *Journalism: State of the Art.* Westport, Conn.: Praeger Publishers.

——. (2003). *The Human Journalist: Reporters, Perspectives, and Emotions.* Afterword by Col. Ann Norwood, M.D., Mary Walsh, and Penny Owen. Westport, Conn.: Praeger Publishers.

Wilson, Clint C., II, and Felix Gutierrez. (1985). *Minorities and Media: Diversity and the End of Mass Communication.* Beverly Hills, Calif.: SAGE Publications.

Wilson, Clint C., II, Felix Gutierrez, and Lena M. Chao. (2003). *Racism, Sexism and the Media: The Rise of Class Communication in Multicultural America.* Thousand Oaks, Calif.: SAGE Publications.

Wingate, Charles F. (1875). *Views and Interviews on Journalism.* New York: F. B. Patterson.

Index

About the Author

Edd Applegate has taught undergraduate and graduate courses in advertising, journalism, and mass communications at Middle Tennessee State University and other colleges and universities. Prior to teaching he worked in public relations for a state educational organization, for which he wrote numerous articles that were published in various newspapers.

Applegate has written several books, including *The Advocacy Journalists: A Biographical Dictionary of Writers and Editors* (2009), *Muckrakers: A Biographical Dictionary of Writers and Editors* (2008), *Strategic Copywriting: How to Create Effective Advertising* (2004), *Personalities and Products: A Historical Perspective on Advertising in America* (1998), and *Literary Journalism: A Biographical Dictionary of Writers and Editors* (1996), to mention a few.

He has contributed numerous chapters and entries to other books and encyclopedias. His scholarly research and book reviews have appeared in *American Journalism, ASJMC INSIGHTS, CHOICE, Feedback, JACA: Journal of the Association for Communication Administration, Journal of Advertising Education, Journalism and Mass Communication Educator, Journalism and Mass Communication Quarterly, Journalism History, Journalism Studies,* and *Public Relations Quarterly,* among other academic journals. Other scholarly research has been presented at academic conferences and published in proceedings, including those published by the American Academy of Advertising and the Marketing Management Association, to mention two.

Applegate has received grants and fellowships from the Freedom Forum Media Studies Center, the Gannett Foundation, the American Association of Advertising Agencies, the American Press Institute, the Donald and Geraldine

Hedberg Foundation, the Direct Marketing Educational Foundation, and other organizations.

He received his doctorate from Oklahoma State University. He has continued his formal education at Pennsylvania State University and Vanderbilt University, among others.

Applegate served as the advisor and publisher to two college newspapers, two yearbooks, and one magazine. He helped develop numerous articles and create hundreds of advertisements for these publications. He has helped more than twenty-five clients in middle Tennessee improve their communications and advertising.

9 780810 881853

DATE DUE